Durance

Focalquier

Manosque

l'Aix
Provence

Massif de la Sainte-
Baume

Toulon

Var

Arrière-Pays Niçois
Vence
Nice

Côte d'Azur

O

E

S

ranée

Provence Interiors
Intérieurs de Provence
Interieurs in der Provence

Lisa Lovatt-Smith

Provence Interiors
Intérieurs de Provence
Interieurs in der Provence

Edited by
Angelika Muthesius

TASCHEN

KÖLN LISBOA LONDON NEW YORK PARIS TOKYO

Erde sich mischen, wo die mit Schilfrohr gedeckten Hütten, die winzigen Fischerkaten und die langgestreckten Reptilien der weißgekalkten »Mas« – der Landhäuser – auf eigenartige Weise mitten im Rhône-Delta an die Ile de Ré erinnern. Auf das Wesentlichste beschränkte Interieurs, düstere, kostbare Möbelstücke, große, weiß-blau karierte Tücher, dazu als einziger Schmuck das Tag für Tag benutzte Werkzeug und das Material, aus dem es gefertigt war, Kupfer, Leder, Roßhaar. Erst nach dem Zweiten Weltkrieg haben Ziergegenstände aus Schmiedeeisen, ausgestopfte Vögel und Fotos oder Bilder der lokalen Künstler die asketisch-aristokratische Kargheit dieser Häuser gebrochen, die aufgrund der äußeren Bedingungen bis dahin unberührt geblieben waren: Schließlich halten Mistral, Mücken und Sümpfe alle fern, außer denen, die es als wirkliche Liebhaber nicht scheuen, beim Licht der Petroleumlampen zu sitzen.

Bis in die sechziger Jahre hinein glaubte ich, mich hier inmitten einer aus der Literatur stammenden Pampa zu befinden, mit den windgetriebenen Schöpfpumpen am Horizont, den in der Sonne brütenden Weilern, apathisch unter dem Staub der gestampften Erde, und den bunt hingestreuten Hütten, gebaut aus Holz, das mit Flößen herbeigeschafft wurde, aus Metallschrott und aus Bruchstücken von armiertem Beton. Die perlmuttfarbenen oder violett schimmernden Seen, der zu geometrischen Mustern zersprungene, ausgetrocknete Boden oder der tintendunkle Schlamm, das blutige Orange der untergehenden Sonne und davor das Lachsrosa der Flamingos – all das gehörte für viele zur exotischen Poesie dieses abgeschlossenen, eigentümlichen Universums der »Bouvine«, der Stier- und Pferdezüchter, von denen manche Kontakt zum damaligen »Jet-set« hatten, so daß bald allerlei Importe in diese natürliche Düsterkeit einbrachen: neogothischer Nippes, Jugendstilmöbel oder – Gipfel des Snobismus – ein botanischer Garten.

Sommer in Fontvieille, Winter in Arles
Das Weiß der Pferde, das Schwarz der Stiere, die Blässe der Gewächse bildeten den »zen-haften«, abstrakten, strengen Grundton dieser schnörkellosen

holy images, starchy portraits, red tiles (*mallons*) underfoot, old stoneware sinks, pools of yellow light, cracked faïence, the mellow ticking of a clock. Everything that has since turned to gold in the hands of the antique merchant was then the stuff of everyday life. *Aficionados* of the bull-ring would indulge themselves with salons of a tauromachic baroque: capes, swords, banderillas and other trophies or relics. The thirties and forties added a zest of solid art deco, the tubby "club" armchair and vast wireless sets. Then the northern fashion for chintz was translated to the south in the form of serially coordinated countryfied cretonnes. A return to the town, where over the tangle of tiled roofs, belvederes and covered or glazed terraces that lines the banks of the Rhône, the horizon is dogtoothed with the limestone belltowers of Arles. Between the 17th and 19th century, houses had retained the often dismal half-dark of Raspal's paintings. Bare stone walls, occasional wainscoting with canvases sometimes pasted directly on to it; the occasional fresco. Paintings black with varnish, lanterns, the furniture of several different generations commingled, sometimes a music room long forgotten behind the penumbra of closed shutters, wide staircases with sinuous wrought-iron balustrades, a certain silence, the certainty of cold. Behind high walls were the hanging gardens with their labyrinthine terraces of trees, damp patches in plenty, a palm tree here, a palm tree there. Ivy, cretonne prints and the trimmings and braids of the fifties and sixties retained some measure of dignity, a certain lofty elegance. The seventies and eighties took a knife to these soft, upholstered, enclosed spaces, bastardized the complexity of volute and scroll, stripped façades to the bone, whitewashed them, rendered the pebble-dash sickly with the obligatory "peach", "almond" and "vanilla", transformed the ground floors into aquariums open to every eye, converted the *souillardes* (sculleries) into "loft / kitchenette / bistrot", and turned the surrounding land into appalling housing estates whose "inspiration" was ignorance, greed or a half-digested modernism.

My nostalgia is not obsessive. I am thrilled by contemporary architecture of talent. It is no less

des iris étaient plantés à même les rues, les trottoirs en «calade» (pierre) de Crau, à l'aplomb des façades qui s'ouvraient de portes à moustiquaires qu'un petit sac de cotonnade lesté de sable au bout d'un cordon à poulie, refermait en jouant les contre-poids, sur des rideaux en lourd filet frangés, plus tard remplacés par les lanières de plastique multicolores des années cinquante et soixante.

Les mêmes cénacles se réunissaient l'hiver au coin des cheminées qui embaumaient la clémentine, le clou de girofle et le vin vieux. Sensualité respectable des meubles de Fourques tout en courbes et arabesques, images saintes, portraits empesés, «mallons» (carreaux) rouges par terre, «pile» (évier) profonde de grès antique, éclairages jaunes un peu chiches, faïences craquelées, tic-tac d'horloge moelleux, fleurs et couleurs des boutis: tout ce répertoire devenu depuis l'or des marchands se vivait au jour le jour. Les aficionados risquaient le baroque d'un salon tauromachique accroché de têtes de «toros», capes, épées, banderilles et autres trophées ou reliques. Les années trente et quarante agrémentèrent ces décors d'un zeste d'Art déco massif, de fauteuils de cuir «club» et d'énormes postes de T.S.F. Puis la mode du chintz, au nord, se traduisit dans le sud par une marée de cretonnes folkloriques coordonnées à l'infini. Retour en ville, avec, à l'horizon, la mâchoire calcaire des clochers arlésiens étalés le long du Rhône dans l'enchevêtrement des toitures de tuiles, des belvédères et des terrasses couvertes ou vitrées. Les maisons XVIIe – XVIIIe et XIXe avaient gardé la pénombre pas forcément gaie des tableaux de Raspal. Murs de pierre nue, à peine quelques lambris ou toiles marouflées, fresques parfois. Des tableaux noircis de vernis, des lanternes, la coexistence des mobiliers de plusieurs générations et même un salon de musique oublié dans l'obscurité, d'amples escaliers à ferronneries sinueuses, un certain silence et un froid certain, des arbres sur des terrasses suspendues en labyrinthes derrière de hauts murs, beaucoup de taches d'humidité, souvent un palmier. Le lierre, la toile de Jouy et les passementeries des années cinquante et soixante avaient conservé une certaine réserve, encore un peu de hauteur et d'élégance. Puis les années

Häuser. Welch ein Kontrast zum vielfarbigen Kitsch der Zigeunerkarren, der »roulottes«, und der sinnlicheren, freundlicheren Opulenz des liebenswürdigen Örtchens Fontvieille, wo wir den Juni zu verbringen pflegten, im Reich der realistisch-idyllischen Geschichten des Schriftstellers und Filmers Marcel Pagnol (und nicht in der versponnen romantischen Provence des Epikers Baroncelli). Hier duftete es süß aus dem Ofen des Bäckers, der Stand des Buchhändlers roch nach feuchter Druckerschwärze, und die Bäche trugen bläuliche Waschlauge fort; alles jedoch war beherrscht von Pinien, Lavendel und Thymian. Die Steine aus den hiesigen Brüchen waren fast so hell wie diejenigen aus Aix, und die stämmigen Dörfer duckten sich unter Platanenalleen, unter Spalieren von wildem Wein und Pergolen voller Glyzinien. Drinnen massige Mauern, einfarbig ockergelb, blau – in einem »Sainte Vierge« genannten Ton – oder pistaziengrün. Die Fensterläden in demselben, etwas an Gauloise-Schachteln erinnernden Hellblau wie der Anstrich der Karren oder in dem Grün, in dem die Gartenmöbel gehalten waren, bevor Weiß als eleganteste Lösung aufkam. Unter den Gewölben empfing man seine Gäste in einem Durcheinander aus Korbmöbeln, Karaffen und Flaschen, ganz wie es an den Sonntagen in den ländlichen Häusern üblich war, den »Cabanons« in der Gegend von Marseille, den »Campagnes« und »Masets« rings um Nîmes oder gar den »Solitudes« auf den einsamen Höhen über Perpignan. In der größten Hitze versuchten die Feigensträucher, allem anderen den Rang abzulaufen, mit ihrem ganz besonderen moschusartigen, milchigen Duft, während aus zu Pflanzgefäßen verwandelten Öl- oder Olivenkübeln Geranien hingen. Nelken und Iris pflanzte man einfach an die Straße oder auf die Bürgersteige – diese waren aus Feldsteinen gesetzt – oder direkt an die Fassaden der Häuser. Als Eingangstür hatte man sommers Fliegengitter, die von einem kleinen, sandgefüllten Baumwollsäckchen zugezogen wurden, es hing als Gegengewicht an einem Strick, der über eine Rolle lief; drinnen Türvorhänge aus schwerem Netzgewebe mit Fransen, das später, in den Fünfzigern und Sechzigern, durch grellbunte Plastikstreifen verdrängt wurde.

soul-destroying to cut oneself off from one's memory than to wall oneself into a sterile and dogmatic tradition of regionalism. When, in 1987, I founded my "Maison de Couture", drawing on my roots to do so, to the rhythm of the Spanish *movida* I was inching open the gate of a secret garden where the music of the Gypsy Kings played. Since then I have often been tempted – pretension or presumption – to think of myself (and not just myself) as a sort of sorcerer's apprentice from whom flowed a tide of fashion that fashion itself made unfashionable. I had walked the soil of Provence to Paris and now Paris was at my coat-tails when I returned to my most intimate landmarks. I had forgotten that "the decisive event cannot be forestalled"; that I was myself carried on that tide, more instrument than *agent provocateur*. So I beat a retreat. My House in the South is a hotel in Arles (the Hôtel du Nord!), my Provence is really the Languedoc and my Camargue is the Petite Camargue on the fringes of my ancestral Cévennes. For now, my Paris is an ivory tower, an observatory from which to observe the year 2000, the Rhône valley and a few supplementary "flashcards": a Pagnolesque *Château de ma mère* – a sort of rustic, Napoléon III style Trianon full of opaline hues – next to Daudet's windmill, the interiors of Christian Bérard, a little hut on stilts, another amongst the trees of Aigues-Mortes, some 16th-century apartments at Baux with their successive terraced gardens, the naive paintings found in café-restaurants, the raw architecture, now endangered, of the Beauduc beachhouses, the Palladian villa in Lambese whose American owner lives, eats and dresses *à la* 18th century, and certain bourgeois residences in the parodic style of Tati. And I recall a succulent property imbued with the arty culture of its British inhabitants who had shown much more respect for it than did the native worthies who succeeded them. The beautiful gardens of Provence are almost always Anglo-Saxon. This is tradition: the Comtat Venaissin, antechamber to Tuscany. For Provence, like England or Italy, possesses the true and original aristocracy, the nobility of land, where the city counts for little. It is a rural, poetic, peasant civilisation remote from salons, out of reach of Parisian or Bovaryiste

snob-soixante-dix et quatre-vingt ont éventré la chair des volumes cloisonnés, abâtardi les circonvolutions complexes, mis à nu, à vif, à blanc les façades ou affadi les crépis avec la gamme obligatoire des «pêche», «amande» et «vanille», transformé les rez-de-chaussée en aquarium, les «souillardes» (arrière-cuisine) en «loft /kitchenette/bistrot», les alentours en lotissements désespérants pour cause d'ignorance, de lucre, ou de modernisme mal digéré.

Je ne suis pas d'une nostalgie pathologique. L'architecture contemporaine m'emballe quand elle a du talent. Et je pense qu'il y a autant de risque à perdre son âme avec sa mémoire, qu'à se retrancher dans le camp stérile du traditionalisme régionaliste. En 1987, au moment de fonder une Maison de Couture sur les bases de mes racines, j'ai entrouvert le portail d'un jardin secret sur la musique des Gypsy Kings et au même rythme que la Movida espagnole; j'ai été depuis souvent tenté d'avoir la prétention ou la présomption de me penser avec d'autres l'apprenti sorcier d'une mode déferlante vite démodable. J'avais charrié la Provence à mes semelles jusqu'à Paris et je traînais en retour Paris à mes basques jusqu'au fin fond de mes repères. C'était oublier que «ce qui est décisif se produit malgré tout» et que j'étais moi-même porté par une vague inéluctable, instrument plus qu'agent provocateur. Alors j'ai battu en retraite. Ma Maison dans le Sud est un hôtel à Arles («l'hôtel du Nord!»), ma Provence, c'est plutôt le Languedoc et ma Camargue, la «Petite» aux limites des Cévennes paternelles. Quant à mon Paris, pour un temps, c'est une tour d'ivoire ou plutôt un observatoire d'où scruter l'an 2000, la vallée du Rhône et quelques «flashes» supplémentaires: un «Château de ma mère», Trianon rustique et le style Napoléon III plein d'opalines à côté du Moulin de Daudet, et les intérieurs de Christian Bérard, une cabane sur pilotis et une autre dans les arbres à Aigues-Mortes, des appartements XVIe aux Baux, avec des jardins en cascade, des cafés-restaurants aux peintures naïves, l'art brut des constructions menacées sur la plage de Beauduc, la villa palladienne de Lambesc où une Américaine vit, mange et s'habille XVIIIe, les résidences à la Tati d'une certaine bourgeoisie. Je me souviens aussi

Im Winter dann fand man sich beim Kamin zusammen, wo es nach Clementinen, Nelkengewürz und altem Wein duftete. Dort war alles vereint, womit man heute für viel Geld Häuser einrichtet: Die respektheischende Sinnlichkeit der Fourques-Möbel, gewundene Arabesken, Heiligenbilder, steife Porträts, am Boden rote Terrakotta, an der Wand tiefe, alte Steinzeug-Schüttsteine, dazu gelbliche, etwas trübe Beleuchtung, Fayence-Keramik, dumpf tickende Standuhren, Blumen und erdige Farben... Begeisterte Stierkampfanhänger leisteten sich recht barock anmutende Wohnzimmer voller ausgestopfter Köpfe der »toros«, voller Capes, Schwerter, Banderillas und anderer Trophäen oder Reliquien. Die dreißiger und vierziger Jahre würzten dieses Dekor mit einer Prise massiver Art deco, mit ledernen »Clubsesseln« und enormen Rundfunkgeräten. Danach schwappte die Chintz-Welle aus dem Norden in den Süden über und bescherte ihm eine Flut aufeinander abgestimmter Kretonne-Folklorestoffe.

Bei der Rückkehr in die Stadt stieg dann am Horizont entlang der Rhône das steinerne Gebiß der Türme von Arles auf, das Gewirr von Ziegeldächern, Erkern und überdachten oder verglasten Terrassen. Die Häuser aus dem 17., 18. und dem 19. Jahrhundert strahlten die nicht gerade fröhliche Düsterkeit der Gemälde eines Raspal aus mit ihren rohen Steinmauern, die nur selten getäfelt oder mit Stoff bespannt, manchmal von Fresken verziert waren: In ihrem Inneren Laternen, ein Durcheinander von Möbeln aus verschiedenen Generationen, hier und da gar ein in der Dunkelheit vergessenes Musikzimmer, Bilder unter dunkelndem Firnis, breite Treppen mit geschwungenem Schmiedewerk, eine gewisse abweisende Stille, viele Stockflecken, hinter hohen Mauern Labyrinthe von baumbestandenen Terrassen, überall Palmen. Waren die fünfziger und sechziger Jahre mit ihrem Efeu, den Tuchen aus Jouy und ihrem Zierat noch von einer gewissen Zurückhaltung, einem Rest von Hochmut und Eleganz geprägt, so rissen die Siebziger und Achtziger die Gebäude auf, ebneten alles Charakteristische ein, stellten das Innere aus, übertünchten alles Dunkel-Intime mit den obligatorischen, pastelligen »Peach«-, »Mandel«- und »Vanille«-Tönen, machten die Erdge-

snobbery. And it is rich too in the enlightened spirit of painters and writers, native or otherwise, who guard Provence from indignities – sometimes, indeed, inflicted by the Provençaux. In this way the West crossbreeds with the East, tosses off its Indian influences or (via Marseille) those of the rest of the Mediterranean, which, if we are to believe Darius Milhaud, extends from Istanbul to Rio de Janeiro, from *moucharabies* to *azulejos*, taking in the Pompeian atrium on its way. And so a distant vision of this "Arles house" is vouchsafed to me: ideal and paradoxical, composite and coherent, mineral and vegetal, traditional and contemporary, cosmopolitan and local, popular and patrician, astonishing yet reassuring; it is respectful, above all, of the history and geography that compose it, living in osmosis with its inhabitant. This is a land that requires respect, a little acre of mythology over which its myriad subterranean deities mount guard.

The houses which follow as if part of a dream village (for Palladio the town is simply a large house and the house a small town) are, each and every one of them, aspects of a very real dream. Formed as each of them were by Provence – that same Provence that moulded my vision of fashion as surfing on the undulations of a landscape perpetually changing through time – the owners have each created their own Provence. The changes within a house, too, should leave it continuous with its former self. "When the dwelling is finished, there Death enters," says the Arab proverb. So let our labours be ever unfinished.

d'une propriété «dans son jus», imprégnée de la culture «artiste» des Britanniques qui l'avaient respectée bien plus que les notables autochtones qui leur succédèrent. Les beaux jardins en Provence sont presque toujours anglo-saxons. Vieille tradition; le Comtat comme antichambre de la Toscane. C'est que la Provence, comme l'Angleterre ou l'Italie, a la noblesse véritable, primitive, celle de la terre, où la campagne compte plus que la ville, civilisation agreste, poète et paysanne, loin des salons, au-delà des snobismes parisianistes ou bovarystes. Et aussi l'esprit éclairé des peintres ou des écrivains de là ou d'ailleurs, garde-fous et garants de la Provence malgré, parfois, les Provençaux. Ainsi l'Occident métisse l'Orient et balance l'influence des Indes ou, via Marseille, du reste de la Méditerranée, qui va, selon Darius Milhaud, d'Istanbul à Rio de Janeiro, des moucharabiehs aux azulejos en passant par l'atrium pompéien. Je commence à l'entrevoir cette «maison-Arlésienne» idéale et paradoxale, composite et cohérente, minérale et végétale, traditionelle et contemporaine, cosmopolite et locale, populaire et patricienne, étonnante et rassurante, respectueuse, surtout de son histoire et de sa géographie qui la dictent, en osmose avec qui l'habite. C'est une terre qui exige le respect, un arpent de mythologie plein de petits dieux souterrains qui veillent.

Toutes les maisons qui vont suivre dans ce livre comme pour former un village de rêve (pour Palladio la ville n'est rien d'autre qu'une grande maison et la maison n'est rien d'autre qu'une petite ville) toutes ces maisons, donc, sont les facettes d'un mirage bien réel. Chaque propriétaire donne sa version de la Provence mais c'est la Provence qui les a eux-mêmes façonnés comme elle a façonné ma vision de la mode surfant sans cesse sur la vague d'un paysage en perpétuelle évolution. Une maison se doit d'être de même, ni tout à fait la même ni tout à fait une autre. «Quand la demeure est finie la Mort entre», dit un proverbe arabe. Ne la finissons donc jamais!

schosse zu Aquarien, die nach hinten gelegenen, »Souillardes« genannten Küchen zu »Lofts«, »Kitchenettes«, »Bistros«, sie verschandelten alles ringsum aus Ignoranz, Gewinnstreben oder halbverdautem Modernismus.

Ich bin nicht krankhaft in alles Vergangene verliebt. Zeitgenössische Architektur kann mich begeistern, wenn Talent in ihr erkennbar ist. Schließlich ist das Risiko, zusammen mit der Erinnerung die eigene Seele zu verlieren, ebenso groß wie die Gefahr, sich auf einen sterilen lokalen Traditionalismus zurückzuziehen. Als ich 1987 meine Maison de Couture gründete, versuchte ich behutsam, einen verwunschenen Garten mit der Musik der Gypsy Kings und dem Rhythmus des spanischen Nachtlebens in Einklang zu bringen. Seitdem versuche ich mich gemeinsam mit anderen in einem Dasein als Zauberlehrling der so mitreißenden wie schnell vergänglichen Mode – ohne Anmaßung oder Dünkel, so will ich hoffen. Ich hatte an meinen Sohlen etwas von der Provence bis nach Paris mitgebracht und in umgekehrter Richtung etwas Pariserisches in das Land meiner Geburt getragen – zu meiner Überraschung, denn ich hatte eine Zeitlang vergessen, daß die Herkunft sich aus eigener Kraft geltend macht und ich selber, von dieser kraftvollen Welle getragen, weniger »Agent provocateur« war als vielmehr ein Instrument. Also habe ich den Rückzug angetreten. Mein Haus im Süden ist ein Hotel in Arles (das »Hôtel du Nord«!). Und meine Träume erfüllen sich mir in doppelter Weise abseits, der Traum von der Provence westlich im Languedoc und der von der Camargue in der »Kleinen Camargue« westlich von Les Saintes-Maries-de-la-Mer am Fuße der Cevennen, aus denen mein Vater stammt. Und was ist dann Paris für mich? Ein Elfenbeinturm? Nein, ein Observatorium, aus dem ich den Blick auf das Jahr 2000 richte, dazu auf das Rhônetal und einige zusätzliche Schlaglichter: Ein »Schloß meiner Mutter« – einer der Romane von Marcel Pagnol –, ein opal schimmerndes Schlößchen in einem zugleich bäuerlichen und an das Second Empire erinnernden Stil neben der Mühle in Fontvieille, wo Alphonse Daudet seine »Briefe aus meiner Mühle« geschrieben hat, und die Interieurs des Malers und Bühnenbildners

Christian Bérard, eine Hütte auf Pfeilern und eine andere auf einem Baum in Aigues-Mortes, Wohnungen aus dem 16. Jahrhundert in Les-Baux-de-Provence mit terrassenartig angelegten Gärten, Café-Restaurants voll naiver Gemälde, ein Blick auf die »Art Brut« der bedrohten Gebäude am Strand von Beauduc, auf die palladianische Villa in Lambesc, in der eine Amerikanerin ganz nach dem Vorbild des 18. Jahrhunderts lebt, auch, was Essen und Kleidung anbelangt, und Residenzen, die einem Film von Jacques Tati zu entstammen scheinen. Ich erinnere mich auch an ein Anwesen »von altem Schrot und Korn«, geprägt von der künstlerischen Kultur der Briten, die ihr Domizil weit mehr respektiert hatten als die ortsansässigen Notabeln, welche auf sie gefolgt waren. Die schönen Gärten der Provence sind fast alle angelsächsischen Ursprungs. Eine alte Tradition: Das Comtat Venaissin, jene fruchtbare Ebene im Dreieck zwischen der Rhône und dem Fluß Durance, als Vorzimmer der Toskana. In der Provence nämlich lebt wie in England oder Italien ein echter, ursprünglicher, erdnaher Adel, für den das Land mehr zählt als die Stadt; eine im guten Sinne bäuerliche, eine ländlich-poetische Zivilisation fern der Salons, unberührt von allem Großstadt-Snobismus. Überdies kommt ihr der wache Geist der Maler und Schriftsteller zugute; ob diese nun hier geboren sind oder von anderen Orten kommen, sie sind die Irrenwärter und Bürgen der Provence, die sie manchmal sogar vor den Provenzalen schützen müssen. So vermischt sich der Okzident mit dem Orient und verdrängt den Einfluß Indiens oder via Marseille den des restlichen Mittelmeerraums, der, wenn man dem Komponisten Darius Milhaud glauben darf, von Istanbul bis nach Rio de Janeiro reicht, von den byzantinischen Muscharabijes, den Holzgittern vor den Fenstern, über die pompejanischen Atrien bis zu den schmuckvollen Azulejo-Kacheln.

Langsam bildet sich in mir eine Vorstellung von jenem idealen und paradoxen Haus, dem Ziel meiner Träume: Es wird zusammengewürfelt und homogen sein, mineralisch und vegetabil, so traditionell wie zeitgenössisch, so volkstümlich wie herrschaftlich, es sollte Überraschung ebenso vermitteln wie Geborgenheit, soll vor allem die Geschichte und die Geographie respektieren, die es ebenso wie seine Bewohner beeinflussen. Die Provence ist ein Land, das respektiert werden will, ein mythischer Garten voll kleiner unterirdischer Schutzgottheiten.

Alle Häuser, die in diesem Buch gezeigt werden, als sollten sie gemeinsam ein Traumdorf bilden (für Palladio ist übrigens die Stadt nichts anderes als ein großes Haus und ein großes Haus nichts als eine kleine Stadt), all diese Häuser sind Teile eines sehr realen Wunschbildes. Jeder ihrer Eigentümer formuliert sein Bild von der Provence, doch die Provence selber hat jeden einzelnen von ihnen geprägt, wie sie meine Vision von der Mode geprägt hat als etwas, das unaufhörlich auf der Welle einer sich ewig wandelnden Landschaft surft. Mit einem Haus muß es ebenso gehen, weder darf es stets unverändert bleiben noch sich von Grund auf ändern. »Wenn das Haus fertig ist, tritt der Tod ein«, sagt ein arabisches Sprichwort. Lassen wir also immer noch etwas zu tun übrig!

Introduction/Einleitung

de / by / von Lisa Lovatt-Smith
Photos: Edouard Boubat

> **"Provence has a thousand faces, a thousand aspects, a thousand characters, and it is wrong to describe it as a single and indivisible phenomenon."**
>
> *Jean Giono*

This may seem a rather dry quote from one of Provence's most celebrated writers, who was as severe as the mountain landscape of the Haute-Provence where he was born. Seen through the prism of contemporary sentimentalism that today determines all reference to the region, voices such as Giono's or even Colette's, who echoed him in bantering "Of course you love Provence – but which Provence?", have been submerged by a single assumption in the spirit of Ford Madox Ford, who described Provence as "paradise on Earth". Fuelled by Peter Mayle's sugary best sellers, enthusiasm for the pastoral delights of the area has now reached a fever pitch. From the Carmargue on the Mediterranean, to Barcelonette in the Alpes-Maritimes, Provence is often perceived as a "single and indivisible phenomenon", a bucolic land of lavender fields and fortified hilltop villages. How Giono would have disapproved!

"Provence" is a purely intellectual, or rather emotional, concept. Its borders have long been disputed, not least by the Provençaux themselves. Occupying all the south-eastern corner of France, the "official" Provence comprises five administrative districts or *départements* which together stretch from the Rhône to the Alps. It includes not only the coast where Colette lived, but also the austere highlands celebrated by Giono. The 1904 Nobel Prize winner Frédéric Mistral, the poet who was instrumental in reviving the lost Provençal tongue and who attracted international attention to his cause, defined it thus: "It was the Rhône that made Provence in concert with the wind. Right bank, left bank, kingdom, empire, all are Provence. Of course, its borders are drawn by the language but also by the prevailing wind: the mistral. Wherever the mistral rules, you are in Provence." This other mistral is none other than the infamous wind with which the poet shared his name and which Stendhal described as "Le grand *drawback* de Provence". It does not blow on the Riviera and so excludes this celebrated coastline

«La Provence présente mille visages, mille facettes, mille personnalités et il est vain de la décrire comme un phénomène unique et indivisible.»

Jean Giono

Voilà une affirmation quelque peu lapidaire de la part de l'un des écrivains les plus célèbres de Provence... aussi sévère que les paysages montagneux de sa Haute-Provence natale. Devant le sentimentalisme qui affleure aujourd'hui dans la moindre allusion à cette région, des voix telles que celles de Giono ou même de Colette, (qui renchérit sur un ton badin: «Bien sûr que tu aimes la Provence, mais quelle Provence?») sont étouffées par celles qui décrivent la Provence comme un paradis terrestre. Alimenté par les best-sellers de l'anglais Peter Mayle, l'engouement pour la région bat aujourd'hui son plein. De la Camargue à la Méditerranée, de Barcelonette aux Alpes-Maritimes, la Provence est souvent perçue comme un «phénomène unique et indivisible», une terre bucolique de champs de lavande et de villages fortifiés perchés à la cime des collines. Giono doit se retourner dans sa tombe!

La «Provence» est un concept purement intellectuel, ou disons plutôt, purement affectif. Ses frontières sont disputées depuis toujours, et pas seulement par les Provençaux. Occupant le Sud-Est de la France, la Provence «officielle» s'étend du Rhône aux Alpes. Elle comprend la Côte d'Azur où Colette a vécu, mais aussi les hauteurs austères célébrées par Giono. Frédéric Mistral, lauréat du prix Nobel en 1904, a fortement contribué à la renaissance de la langue provençale et à attirer l'attention du monde entier sur sa cause: «Mais c'est le Rhône qui a fait la Provence, d'accord avec le vent. Rive droite, rive gauche, royaume, empire, tout cela c'est la Provence. Elle est délimitée encore, bien entendu, par la langue, mais aussi par le vent maître: le mistral. Partout où il règne, vous êtes en Provence.» Ce redoutable vent auquel le poète doit son nom n'avait pas les faveurs de Stendhal, qui le qualifiait de «grand inconvénient de la Provence». Il ne sévit pas sur la Côte d'Azur, ce qui exclut le célèbre littoral de la définition de Mistral. D'ailleurs, la différence est notable: l'esthétique de la Côte d'Azur est le fruit

»Die Provence hat tausend Gesichter, tausend Aspekte, tausend Charaktere, und es ist falsch, sie als ein einziges, unteilbares Phänomen darzustellen.«

Jean Giono

Dieser Satz aus der Feder eines der berühmtesten provenzalischen Schriftsteller mag recht trocken klingen, ebenso streng wie die Berglandschaft der Haute-Provence, wo er geboren wurde. Wenn man die Dinge nur im Licht der sentimentalen Attitüde sieht, die die meisten derzeitigen Äußerungen über diese Region prägt, werden Stimmen wie die Gionos oder Colettes, die mit ihrer scherzhaften Frage: »Natürlich lieben Sie die Provence – nur welche Provence?«, den gleichen Standpunkt vertrat, durch ein einziges pauschales Urteil wie das von Ford Madox Ford vom Tisch gewischt; dieser nämlich nannte die Provence das »Paradies auf Erden«. Bestärkt durch Peter Mayles süßliche Bestseller hat die Begeisterung für bukolische Genüsse mittlerweile den Siedepunkt erreicht. Die Provence, von der Camargue am Mittelmeer bis Barcelonette in den Alpes-Maritimes, wird oft als »ein einziges, unteilbares Phänomen«, als Land der Hirten, der Lavendelfelder und befestigten Bergdörfer begriffen.

Die »Provence« existiert lediglich als rein intellektuelle oder eher noch als emotionale Vorstellung. Ihre tatsächlichen Grenzen sind seit langem umstritten, nicht zuletzt bei den *provençaux* selbst. Die »offizielle« Provence in der südöstlichen Ecke Frankreichs umfaßt fünf Verwaltungsbezirke oder Départements, die sich von der Rhône bis zu den Alpen erstrecken. Dazu gehört nicht nur die Küste, an der Colette lebte, sondern auch das von Giono so gepriesene, karge Hochland. Frédéric Mistral, Dichter und Nobelpreisträger von 1904, der maßgeblich an der Wiederbelebung der fast verlorenen provenzalischen Sprache beteiligt war und die Aufmerksamkeit der internationalen Öffentlichkeit auf sein Anliegen richtete, meinte: »Doch es war die Rhône, die der Provence ihr Gesicht gab, zusammen mit dem Wind. Rechtes Ufer, linkes Ufer, Königreich, Kaiserreich, all das ist die Provence. Natürlich sind ihre Grenzen bis heute auch durch die Sprache gekennzeichnet, vor allem aber durch den vorherr-

from Mistral's definition. The aesthetics of the Côte d'Azur are the fruit of five centuries of Italian occupation, and above all else it is the influence of the Mediterranean that dominates the lifestyle and the cuisine there.

The mistral does, however, blow in the Roman town of Nîmes, now part of the *département* of the Gard and no longer "officially" Provence. What is more, Nîmes was the birthplace of Mistral's great friend, Alphonse Daudet, who could not possibly be considered as anything less than a Provençal writer! Mistral's

> "Empire of delight and exhilaration,
> Imaginary Empire of Provence
> Mere mention of your name enchants the
> world!"

thus included the western bank of the river Rhône, historically a great barrier.

Ford Madox Ford called Provence "a highway along which travelled continually the stream of the arts, of thought, of the traditions of life". Although united and part of France since the end of the 15th century it has remained decentralized and inimitable, a sum of all its different parts. Life in Provence reflects the imperatives of rural existence and is thus closely linked to the diversity of its landscape. Giono estimated that in a day's travelling across the region one would come across as many as five hundred different landscapes – and ways of living.

For Jean Giono, born in Manosque in 1895, the solitary life of the shepherds, migrating with the seasons, or of the villagers from the highlands near Forcalquier and Sisteron embodied the true expression of Provence. Their reality was far removed from the cardboard image of nature at its most Arcadian that other writers have evoked. It must be said, however, that in his own way Giono had an equally romanticized vision of rustic existence: something along the lines of the Puritan ideal of redemption through toil, struggle, silence and abstinence. His was perhaps a literary reaction to the ravages of the industrial age and a presentiment of what was to come. His entire *œuvre* is a moving homage to the Haute-Provence. "The highlands are disconcerting... The violence of this part of Provence has held neigh-

de cinq siècles d'occupation italienne, et c'est avant tout l'influence de la Méditerranée qui domine dans son art de vivre et sa cuisine.

En revanche, le mistral souffle sur la ville romaine de Nîmes, désormais rattachée au département du Gard et non plus à la Provence «officielle». En outre, Nîmes est la ville natale du grand ami de Mistral, Alphonse Daudet, que l'on peut difficilement considérer autrement que comme un grand auteur provençal!
La Provence de Mistral,

«Empire de plaisance et d'allégresse,
Empire fantastique de Provence
Qui avec ton nom seul charme le monde!»

s'étend donc outre le Rhône, depuis toujours grande ligne de partage, et inclut sa rive ouest.

Ford Madox Ford a défini la Provence comme «une grande route empruntée de tous temps par le courant des arts, de la pensée et des traditions». Bien qu'intégrée à la France depuis la fin du XVe siècle, elle a gardé son individualité. La vie provençale reflète les impératifs du monde rural et elle est donc étroitement liée à la diversité de son relief. Giono estimait qu'en traversant la région en une journée, on rencontrait près de cinq cents types de paysages différents ... et autant de façons de vivre.

Pour Jean Giono, né à Manosque en 1895, l'existence solitaire des bergers transhumants ou des habitants des villages haut perchés de Forcalquier et de Sisteron était la véritable expression de la Provence. Leur réalité est bien loin de l'image d'Epinal évoquée par d'autres écrivains. Cela dit, la vision de Giono n'est pas dénuée d'un certain romantisme: elle est imprégnée d'une sorte d'idéal puritain de la rédemption par le dur labeur, le combat quotidien pour la survie, le silence et l'abstinence. Sans doute était-ce une réaction littéraire aux ravages de l'ère industrielle, un pressentiment des bouleversements à venir. Son œuvre toute entière est un vibrant hommage à la Haute-Provence: «Les hautes terres déroutent ... La violence de cet endroit de Provence en a écarté les voisins et les caravanes. Il a gardé sa pureté préhistorique et c'est elle qui brusquement vous pousse sur des nouveaux chemins. On n'est jamais venu regarder la Provence

schenden Wind: den Mistral. Überall dort, wo er weht, befinden Sie sich in der Provence.« Dieser andere Mistral, mit dem der Dichter den Namen teilte, ist jener fürchterliche Wind, den Stendhal »le grand *drawback*« – den großen Nachteil – der Provence nannte. An der Riviera weht er nicht, damit ist die vielgepriesene Küste nach Mistrals Definition ausgeschlossen. Es gibt tatsächlich Unterschiede, denn die Schönheiten der Côte d'Azur sind das Erbe einer fünf Jahrhunderte dauernden italienischen Besatzungszeit: hier prägt der Mittelmeerraum Lebensart und Küche.

Der Mistral weht allerdings in der römischen Stadt Nîmes, die heute zum Département du Gard gehört und damit nicht mehr zur »offiziellen« Provence. Außerdem wurde in Nîmes Mistrals bester Freund Alphonse Daudet geboren, ein provenzalischer Schriftsteller *par excellence*. Mistrals Zeilen

»Reich der Freuden und der Fröhlichkeit,
Phantastisches Reich der Provence,
Schon dein Name bezaubert die Welt!«

schlossen insofern das Westufer der Rhône mit ein, die historisch immer die Trennlinie gebildet hat.

Ford Madox Ford nannte die Provence eine »Autobahn, auf der ein kontinuierlicher Strom von Kunstwerken, Gedanken und Traditionen reiste«. Auch nach der Vereinigung und Eingliederung ins französische Reich im 15. Jahrhundert widersetzte sich die Provence der Zentralisierung und blieb unverwechselbar, die Summe ihrer Einzelteile. Das Leben in der Provence spiegelt die Zwänge des bäuerlichen Daseins und ist deshalb eng mit der jeweiligen Landschaft verknüpft. Giono meinte, bei einer Tagesreise durch die Region begegne man wohl bis zu fünfhundert verschiedenen Landschaften – und Lebensweisen.

Für Jean Giono, der 1895 in Manosque geboren wurde, war das einsame Leben der Hirten auf den Sommerweiden oder der Dörfler im Hochland nahe Forcalquier und Sisteron der wahre Inbegriff der Provence. Ihre Realität ist weit entfernt von dem kitschigen Bild einer arkadischen Natur, das andere Autoren malten. Man muß allerdings zugeben, daß Giono selbst eine nicht minder romantische Sicht des bäuerlichen Lebens vertrat, die sich vage am

Une roulotte de gitans

Cette roulotte haute en couleurs est l'un des dernières que l'on
puisse voir en Provence, lieu de passage traditionnel des gitans.
L'idée romantique qu'on se fait d'une vie bucolique de bohémiens,
allant de par les routes dans une jolie petite roulotte telle que
celle-ci, est vite dissipée lorsqu'on se rend au pèlerinage gitan des
Saintes-Maries-de-la-Mer. Ces voyageurs modernes préfèrent désormais le confort des caravanes motorisées. En outre, la tradition
très répandue de brûler la roulotte de famille à la mort d'un des
membres du couple, fait que très peu de modèles anciens sont
parvenus jusqu'à nous. Celle-ci appartient à «Boy», un guitariste
gitan. Construite à Manosque, elle est en tôle et en bois. Dans le
monde entier, les gitans tendent à se sédentariser et Boy n'échappe
pas à la règle. Avec le cheval qui la tirait, cette roulotte a récem-
ment élu domicile sur la route qui mène des Saintes-Maries-de-la-
Mer à Aigues-Mortes, ce segment de route que Van Gogh aimait
tant peindre.

This caravan is particularly small, and yet traditionally would have lodged a family of four or five. The inside of the caravan features two dressers for storage, a raised bed and a small wood-burning stove. The lace curtains at the windows are typical of gypsy interiors.

Particulièrement petite, cette roulotte aurait autrefois accueilli une famille de quatre ou cinq personnes. L'intérieur de la roulotte comporte deux commodes pour le rangement, un lit surélevé et un petit poêle à charbon. Les rideaux en dentelle sont typiques des intérieurs gitans.

Der Wohnwagen ist winzig; trotzdem hätte darin früher eine vier- bis fünfköpfige Familie gelebt. Im Innern des Wohnwagens befinden sich zwei Schränke, ein erhöhtes Bett und ein kleiner Holzofen. Die Spitzenvorhänge vor den Fenstern sind typisch für Zigeunerwagen.

Above: *Denys' bedroom and study where he writes his books and screenplays. It is also home to what he refers to as "the world's most beautiful collection of objects of no value".*
Facing page: *a view of Florian's kitchen. Florian is dedicated to the protection of the ranch's traditional way of life and has chosen to preserve it by opening a charming, if simple, hotel on the property.*

Ci-dessus: *la chambre et le bureau de Denys, où il écrit ses livres et ses scénarios. Elle accueille également ce qu'il appelle «la plus belle collection du monde d'objets sans valeur».*
Page de droite: *la cuisine de Florian. Très attaché à la protection du mode de vie traditionnel du mas, Florian a choisi de le préserver en ouvrant un hôtel simple et charmant sur la propriété.*

Oben: *Denys' Schlaf- und Arbeitszimmer, in dem er seine Bücher und Drehbücher schreibt. Es beherbergt darüber hinaus das, was er selbst »der Welt schönste Sammlung völlig wertloser Gegenstände« nennt.*
Rechte Seite: *ein Blick in Florians Küche. Florian widmet sich mit großem Eifer dem Erhalt der traditionellen Lebensweise auf dem Hof und führt zu diesem Zweck ein zwar einfaches, jedoch sehr gemütliches Hotel auf dem Anwesen.*

Jean Lafont breeds black bulls, hundreds of them; his herd, called "manade" in Provençal, is the oldest in Camargue and has been supplying Provençal bullfights since 1851 when it was founded by the Combet family. However, he is not just a bullfighting man. He is also the Director of the Nîmes opera house, a discerning collector and a celebrated horticulturalist. His home, where he has been living since 1963, is an extraordinary place, decorated and furnished with the help of Marie-Laure de Noailles. An aristocratic patron of the arts, she was both muse and financial backer to artists such as Man Ray, Le Corbusier and Balthus, thus playing a key role in the development of the avant-garde in France before and after the Second World War. Jean Lafont was a collector in his own right from the age of 20 and his house is a homage to his passion, being stuffed with incredibly varied pieces, so that every suite of rooms represents a particular style. The illustration below shows a detail of one of the century-old plane trees that surround the house.

Jean Lafont

Jean Lafont élève les taureaux noirs par centaines. Sa manade est la plus ancienne de Camargue et approvisionne les férias de Provence depuis 1851, date de sa création par la famille Combet. Toutefois, son activité ne s'arrête pas là: il est également directeur de i'opéra de Nîmes, collectionneur avisé et horticulteur renommé. La maison où il vit depuis 1963 est un lieu extraordinaire, décoré et meublé avec l'aide de Marie-Laure de Noailles. Cette mécène aristocratique, à la fois muse et soutien financier d'artistes tels que Man Ray, Le Corbusier et Balthus, a joué un rôle clef dans le développement de l'avant-garde en France avant et après la Seconde Guerre mondiale. Jean Lafont était collectionneur dès l'âge de 20 ans et sa maison est un hommage à sa passion: elle est pleine à craquer d'une incroyable variété d'objets, chaque enfilade de pièces représentant un style particulier. Le détail ci-dessous montre l'un des platanes centenaires qui entourent la maison.

Jean Lafont züchtet schwarze Stiere, und zwar zu Hunderten. Seine Herde, hier »manade« genannt, ist die älteste der Camargue und stellt seit ihrer Gründung 1851 durch die Familie Combet Tiere für provenzalische Stierkämpfe bereit. Lafont selbst ist jedoch nicht einfach nur ein stierkampfbegeisterter Züchter, sondern zudem Leiter des Opernhauses von Nîmes, ein anspruchsvoller Kunstsammler und renommierter Gartenexperte. Sein Haus, in dem er seit 1963 lebt, ist ein außergewöhnliches Gebäude, das er mit Hilfe von Marie-Laure de Noailles gestaltete und einrichtete. Als aristokratische Kunstmäzenin war sie Muse und zugleich finanzieller Rückhalt für Künstler wie Man Ray, Le Corbusier und Balthus und spielte damit eine zentrale Rolle in der Entwicklung der französischen Avantgarde vor und nach dem zweiten Weltkrieg. Jean Lafont ist seit seinem zwanzigsten Lebensjahr ein eigenwilliger Kunstsammler, und sein Haus belegt diese Leidenschaft mit einem Sammelsurium der verschiedensten Stücke. Jeder Raum des Hauses präsentiert sich in einem anderen Stil. Das Detail unten zeigt eine der jahrhundertealten Platanen, die das Haus umgeben.

Above and right: the art nouveau "Green Room", one of the three bedrooms on the first floor. The ceramic fireplace is by Muller and the "honeysuckle" wallpaper was designed by William Morris.

Ci-dessus et à droite: la chambre verte Art nouveau, l'une des trois chambres à coucher du premier étage. La cheminée en céramique est signée Muller et le papier peint «Chèvrefeuille» a été dessiné par William Morris.

Oben und rechts: das im Jugendstil eingerichtete »grüne Zimmer«, einer der drei Schlafräume im ersten Stock. Der aus Keramik gefertigte Kamin ist von Muller, die »Geißblatt«-Tapete ein Entwurf von William Morris.

On the previous pages: *a view of the spectacular glass conservatory, partly designed by the French sculptor César. The porcelain furniture is Sèvres, designed by a disciple of the painter Alfons Mucha. Beyond the conservatory lies the garden, internationally recognized as one of the finest examples of its kind.*
Above: *This room is entirely conceived in the "Gothic revival" style and pays homage to the "dilettante" 18th-century English collector Horace Walpole and his home Strawberry Hill.*
Detail right: *the Gothic bathroom.*

Double page précédente: *le somptueux jardin d'hiver, dessiné en partie par le sculpteur César. Le mobilier en porcelaine a été créé par un élève du peintre Alphonse Mucha pour la manufacture de Sèvres. Derrière, on aperçoit le jardin, un des plus beaux modèles du genre, qui s'étend jusqu'aux prés où paissent les taureaux.*
Ci-dessus: *Cette chambre est entièrement «Gothic revival», un hommage à Horace Walpole, collectionneur dilettante du XVIIIe siècle, et à sa maison Strawberry Hill.*
Détail à droite: *la salle de bains néo-gothique.*

Vorhergehende Doppelseite: *Blick in den prachtvollen, verglasten Wintergarten, der teilweise von dem französischen Bildhauer César entworfen wurde. Die Möbel aus Porzellan wurden in Sèvres nach Entwürfen eines Schülers des Malers Alfons Mucha gearbeitet. Hinter dem Wintergarten erstreckt sich der Garten – einer der schönsten seiner Art.*
Oben: *Dieser Raum ist vollständig im neugotischen Stil gehalten und ist eine Hommage an Horace Walpole, den englischen Kunstliebhaber und -sammler des 18. Jahrhunderts, und an sein Schloß Strawberry Hill.*
Detail rechts: *das neugotische Badezimmer.*

Provence Interiors   Jean Lafont

A view of the Héctor-Guimard-style salon, conceived to evoke the curvy aesthetics beloved of the man who designed the Paris metro entrances. It doubles as a library and office and includes Marie-Laure's mother's fine collection of rare books.
On the following pages: a view of the kitchen. Some of the furniture is by Jacques Majorelle, purchased from film director Louis Malle.

Le salon de style Héctor Guimard, qui évoque l'esthétique tout en courbes du créateur des entrées de métro parisien. Il sert également de bibliothèque et de bureau, et accueille la belle collection de livres rares de la mère de Marie-Laure.
Double page suivante: la cuisine. Certains des meubles sont signés Jacques Majorelle et ont été rachetés au cinéaste Louis Malle.

Blick in den Salon im Stil Héctor Guimards. Er greift die verschlungenen Linien auf, die Guimard bei der Gestaltung der Pariser Metroeingänge so gern verarbeitete. Der Raum dient als Bibliothek und zugleich als Büro und enthält wundervolle, seltene Bücher aus der Sammlung von Maire-Laures Mutter.
Folgende Doppelseite: Blick in die Küche. Einige der Möbel stammen von Jacques Majorelle; Lafont erwarb sie von dem französischen Filmregisseur Louis Malle.

On the slopes of those craggy little mountains know as the Alpilles, the Pellens raise fine horses, which are then bought and exported as far afield as Britain and Germany. Gerald Pellen has horses in his blood and is known not only as an excellent breeder but also as one of the best "rejoneadores" in Provence. He has recently initiated his daughter Patricia into the art of mounted bullfighting and she is one of the very few women to be recognized as a "rejoneadora". On a "corrida" day, a day when bullfights are held, father and daughter dress up in the traditional costume, and travel with their horses to whichever local town is staging the "feria". Pellen has even been accorded the rare honour, as a Provençal, of being invited to display his talents in Spain, home of all bullfighting. At Pellen's family-run stables life is lived according to the needs of the horses: caring for them, breaking them in, training them or practising in the small bullring on the farm, pitting highly strung throughbreds against young bulls.

Gerald Pellen

On vient d'Angleterre et d'Allemagne pour acheter les beaux chevaux des Pellen élevés sur les versants escarpés des Alpilles. Gerald Pellen a les chevaux dans le sang. Ce n'est pas seulement un excellent éleveur mais également le meilleur «rejoneador» de Provence. Il a initié sa fille Patricia à l'art de toréer à cheval et c'est l'une des rares femmes à s'être imposée dans cette profession. Les jours de corrida, on peut voir père et fille faire leur entrée en tenue traditionnelle et accompagnés de leurs montures dans la ville qui accueille la féria. Pellen a même eu le grand honneur, rare pour un Provençal, d'être invité à montrer ses talents en Espagne, patrie de la tauromachie. Dans les écuries des Pellen, la vie est réglée en fonction des besoins des chevaux: il faut les bouchonner, les dresser et les entraîner sur la petite arène du haras, où des pur-sang très nerveux rencontrent de jeunes taureaux.

An den Hängen des zerklüfteten kleinen Alpilles-Gebirges züchtet die Familie Pellen Rassepferde, die bis nach Großbritannien und Deutschland verkauft werden. Gerald Pellen liegen Pferde sozusagen im Blut. Er ist nicht nur ein erfolgreicher Züchter, sondern außerdem auch einer der besten »rejoneadores« der Provence. Auch seine Tochter Patricia hat er in die Kunst des berittenen Stierkampfes eingeführt. Sie wurde als eine von sehr wenigen Frauen mittlerweile selbst als »rejoneadora« zugelassen. Wenn eine Corrida ansteht, ziehen Vater und Tochter die traditionellen Trachten an und fahren mit ihren Pferden zu dem jeweiligen Ort, wo die »feria« stattfindet. Pellen wurde sogar eingeladen, in Spanien, dem Mutterland des Stierkampfes, seine Künste vorzuführen – eine für einen Provenzalen erstaunliche Ehre. In den von der Familie Pellen geführten Ställen orientiert sich das Leben ganz an den Bedürfnissen der Pferde. Man füttert und pflegt sie, reitet sie zu, trainiert sie oder übt in der kleinen Arena auf dem Hof, wo man nervöse Vollblüter gegen junge Stiere antreten läßt.

Above: the entrance hall, where boots and hunting guns stand next to the door, and where trophies and the elaborately decorated "banderillas" are displayed.
Detail right: Patricia's bullfighting costume, a traditional tight-fitting jacket and tie.

Ci-dessus: on dépose ses bottes et ses fusils de chasse près de la porte de l'entrée, où sont exposés trophées et banderilles ouvragées.
Détail de droite: la tenue de «rejoneadora de Patricia», une veste cintrée et une cravate.

Oben: die Eingangshalle, wo Stiefel und Jagdgewehre direkt neben der Tür stehen und wo Trophäen sowie die prächtig dekorierten Banderillas zur Schau gestellt werden.
Detail rechts: Patricias Stierkampfkostüm. Es besteht aus einer eng anliegenden Jacke und einer Krawatte.

The bedroom on the first floor, decorated with florid posters advertising different "corridas". Gerald's bullfighter's cape in the traditional bright pink and deep yellow echoes the ancient "souleiado" bedspread.

La chambre du premier étage, décorée d'affiches de corridas. La cape traditionnelle rose vif et jaune sombre de Gerald est en harmonie avec le «souleiado» ancien du dessus-de-lit.

Im Schlafzimmer im ersten Stock hängen grellbunte Plakate mit Ankündigungen diverser Corridas. Geralds Stierkampfcape, traditionell in leuchtendem Pink und Gelb, paßt zum alten »Souleiado«-Bettüberwurf.

Conran is undoubtedly one of the most important influences on the aesthetics of contemporary interiors. Since he opened the first Habitat in London in 1964, and with his instinctive taste for good, strong design in the home, he has changed the way people perceive decoration. Conran managed to impose a "continental" aesthetic on the insular English in the sixties. France, and the South in particular, has long been an inspiration. The beautifully restored "Mas de Brunélys" near Tarascon is an excercise in "savoire-vivre": very French but very Conran. The house was built in the early 19th century to the design of an Italian count, who endowed the construction with a particular graciousness. The Conrans bought it with 200 acres of olive groves and arable land, which they still allow to be cultivated by the local farmer.

Sir Terence Conran

L'Anglais Sir Terence Conran est sans doute l'un de ceux qui ont le plus influencé la décoration contemporaine. Depuis l'ouverture du premier Habitat en 1964 à Londres, son sens inné d'un design aux lignes fortes a transformé la manière dont les gens conçoivent leurs intérieurs. Dans les années soixante, il est parvenu à imposer une esthétique «continentale» aux Anglais pourtant insulaires. La France et le Sud en particulier, l'inspirent depuis longtemps. Le superbe Mas de Brunélys qu'il a restauré près de Tarascon est une leçon de savoir-vivre, à la fois très français et très «Conran». La maison a été construite au début du XIXe siècle selon les plans d'un comte italien qui a su lui insuffler une certaine grâce. Les Conran l'ont achetée avec 80 hectares d'oliveraies et de terre arable, qui sont encore cultivées par un fermier de la région.

Conran gehört zweifellos zu den Designern, die großen Einfluß auf die zeitgenössische Innenarchitektur ausüben. Seit er 1964 das erste Habitat-Geschäft in London eröffnete, hat er mit seinem Instinkt für gutes, kraftvolles Wohndesign die Rolle der Innenarchitektur nachhaltig verändert. In den sechziger Jahren gelang es Conran, den Briten die »kontinentale« Ästhetik nahezubringen. Frankreich, vor allem der Süden, ist für ihn seit langem eine Quelle der Inspiration. Der wunderschön restaurierte Mas de Brunélys in der Nähe von Tarascon ist ein Modell des »Savoir-vivre«, sehr französisch und zugleich eindeutig ein Conran. Das Haus wurde im frühen 19. Jahrhundert nach Entwürfen eines italienischen Grafen erbaut, der ihm eine ausgesprochen anmutige Note verlieh. Die Conrans kauften das Anwesen zusammen mit 80 Hektar Olivenhainen und Ackerland, die nach wie vor von einem Bauern des Dorfes bewirtschaftet werden.

Page 91: a view of the ochre dining-room with its chandelier improvised out of tri-coloured lanterns.

On the previous pages: a view of the pink salon, in the last of the evening sunlight. The large comfortable sofas are covered in striped mattress ticking. The floor is in the rounded pebbles typical of the region. The two stone fountains on either side of the fireplace are Renaissance.

Above and facing page: two views of the master bedroom, with its periwinkle blue walls and the ancient red tiled floor. The alcove, which was also an original feature of the house, contains a large table with a quilted Provençal "boutis" thrown over it.

Page 91: la salle à manger ocre avec son lustre improvisé avec des lanternes tricolores.

Double page précédente: le salon rose sous les derniers feux du coucher de soleil. Les grands sofas profonds sont recouverts de toile à matelas rayée. Le sol est incrusté de galets de la région. Les deux fontaines en pierre de chaque côté de la cheminée datent de la Renaissance.

Ci-dessus et page de droite: la chambre de maître, avec ses murs bleu pervenche et son sol en tomettes anciennes. L'alcôve, également d'origine, accueille une grande table sur laquelle est jeté un boutis provençal matelassé.

Seite 91: Blick in das ockerfarbene Eßzimmer. Der Kerzenleuchter ist aus dreifarbigen Laternen zusammengesetzt.

Vorhergehende Doppelseite: Blick in den rötlichen Salon im letzten Sonnenlicht. Die ausladenden, gemütlichen Sofas sind mit gestreiftem Matratzendrillich bezogen. Der Fußboden besteht aus den für diese Gegend typischen runden Kieseln. Die beiden Steinbecken rechts und links des Kamins sind echte Renaissancestücke.

Oben und rechte Seite: Zwei Ansichten des Elternschlafzimmers mit den blauvioletten Wänden und dem alten roten Fliesenboden. Der Alkoven gehörte zur Originaleinrichtung des Hauses und enthält einen großen Tisch, über den ein provenzalischer »Boutis«-Quilt gebreitet ist.

Facing page: *a view of the blue and white "chess-board" bathroom, situated in an alcove off the master bedroom. The free-standing bath has improvised curtains made of antique embroidered linen sheets.*
Above: *the guest bedroom, housed in what used to be the stable.*

Page de gauche: *la salle de bains en damier bleu et blanc, nichée dans une alcôve de la chambre de maître. Les rideaux improvisés de la baignoire sur pieds sont d'anciens draps de lin brodés.*
Ci-dessus: *la chambre d'amis dans l'ancienne écurie.*

Linke Seite: *Blick in das blauweiß gewürfelte Badezimmer, das in einer Nische hinter dem Schlafzimmer liegt. Die freistehende Wanne hat improvisierte Vorhänge aus alten bestickten Leinenbahnen.*
Oben: *das Gästezimmer im früheren Stall.*

This rural "mas" lies not far from Tarascon, the celebrated birthplace of the imaginary Tartarin de Tarascon (the writer Alphone Daudet's comic pastiche of the Provençal rustic). Here, a well-known Parisian restaurateur has created a romantic bolt-hole, buried among the orchards of this particularly pretty corner of the lowlands. The inherent simplicity of the house has intentionally been left to shine through. The walls are limewashed with veils of intense colour, but the uneven floors, rough plaster, stairs worn down by many years of footsteps, and the irregular stone work have been allowed to remain, infusing the house with a charm all of its own. The restoration was essentially a case of peeling away layers of previous attempts at decoration in order to reveal the bones of the 18th-century structure.

Un mas en Provence

Ce mas de campagne se trouve près de Tarascon, lieu de naissance du fameux Tartarin, ce rustre provençal imaginé par Alphonse Daudet. Sa propriétaire, une célèbre restauratrice parisienne, en a fait un refuge romantique, enfoui entre les vergers de ce petit coin particulièrement charmant des basses terres. Elle a choisi de préserver la simplicité inhérente à la bâtisse: si les murs ont été passés à la chaux avec un voile de couleurs intenses, les parquets inégaux, le plâtre brut, les escaliers usés par le temps et la maçonnerie grossière sont restés tels quels, conférant à la maison un charme bien particulier. La restauration a simplement consisté à ôter les unes après les autres les tentatives de décoration précédentes afin de mettre à nu les murs du XVIIIe siècle.

Der bäuerliche »mas« liegt ganz in der Nähe von Tarascon, dem berühmten Geburtsort der Romanfigur Tartarin, Alphonse Daudets komischer Parodie auf die provenzalischen Bauern. Hier, in diesem besonders schönen Teil der Ebene, hat eine bekannte Pariser Gastronomin sich zwischen Obstgärten einen romantischen Schlupfwinkel geschaffen. Bewußt wurde bei der Restaurierung die ursprüngliche Schlichtheit des Hauses bewahrt. Die Wände sind mit Kalkfarben in satten Tönen gestrichen, doch die unebenen Fußböden, der Rauhputz, die in langen Jahren von vielen Füßen abgetretene Treppe und das unregelmäßige Mauerwerk wurden belassen und geben dem Haus einen ganz eigenen Charme. Die Restaurierungsarbeiten bestanden im wesentlichen darin, diverse Schichten früherer Dekorationen abzukratzen, um darunter das »Gerippe« des aus dem 18. Jahrhundert stammenden Gebäudes freizulegen.

On the previous pages: *the canary-yellow kitchen showing the fireplace that is dated 1760.*
Above: *the master bedroom, built in what was the hayloft. It occupies the same volume of space as the living room, which is directly underneath it and was in turn converted from the stables. The cupboard doors and the partition separating the bathroom from the rest of the room are made from the recycled wooden blinds of a local chateau.*

Double page précédente: *la cuisine jaune canari et la cheminée qui date de 1760.*
Ci-dessus: *la chambre de maître installée dans l'ancien grenier à foin. Elle occupe le même volume que le salon, situé juste en dessous dans ce qui étaient autrefois les écuries. Les portes des placards et la cloison qui séparent la salle de bains de la chambre sont d'anciens volets en bois provenant d'un château des environs.*

Vorhergehende Doppelseite: *Die kanariengelbe Küche besitzt noch einen Originalkamin aus dem Jahr 1760.*
Oben: *Das Schlafzimmer wurde im ehemaligen Heuboden eingerichtet und ist genauso geräumig wie das unmittelbar darunter gelegene Wohnzimmer, das seinerseits den Platz eines früheren Stalls einnimmt. Für die Schranktüren und die Trennwände zwischen dem Bad und dem übrigen Raum wurden hölzerne Fensterläden eines nahe gelegenen Schlosses verwendet.*

Above: *a view of the permanently cluttered library showing a selection of amusing curiosities.*
Facing page: *a table displaying ceramic vases and a drawing by Picasso.*
On the following pages: *a view of the living room, showing the forties' armchairs and an iron "toro de fuego" bought in Perpignan which observes the aspiring artists sitting at the wide oak table ready to draw the garden view.*
Pages 118/119: *a view into the kitchen.*

Ci-dessus: *la bibliothèque, avec son désordre savant d'objets drôles et inattendus.*
Page de droite: *une nature morte avec des vases en céramique et un dessin de Picasso.*
Double page suivante: *le salon, avec des fauteuils des années quarante. Le «toro de fuego» en fer acheté à Perpignan observe les aspirants artistes qui s'asseoient à la grande table en chêne pour croquer le jardin.*
Pages 118/119: *une vue de la cuisine.*

Oben: *ein Blick in die stets unordentliche Bibliothek mit einer Sammlung interessanter Kuriositäten.*
Rechte Seite: *ein Stilleben mit Keramikvasen und einer Zeichnung von Picasso.*
Folgende Doppelseite: *Blick ins Wohnzimmer mit Lehnstühlen aus den vierziger Jahren und einem eisernen »toro de fuego«, den Grange in Perpignan erwarb und der die Künstler in spe am großen Eichentisch beobachtet, wenn sie dabei sind, das Gartenpanorama zu zeichnen.*
Seiten 118/119: *ein Blick in die Küche.*

The fashion designer Michel Klein, who now designs the couture collection for Guy Laroche, is internationally recognized as a modernist, and his collections are often exercises in purity: monochromatic and sober. In marked contrast to his fashion work, he is a great believer in colour as an essential decorative element for interiors. In his Provençal retreat near Arles he has chosen a different, luminous tone for each room. With the enthusiasm of a child spoilt for choice before a box of finger paints, he daubed his restored "mas" in fuchsia, canary yellow, a vibrant red, emerald green and a blue-mauve that changes colour with the light. In fact he confesses that the most exciting moment in the whole project was choosing the colours from the rainbow of pigments available at Sennelier in Paris. This audacious mix has worked perfectly, opening up the low, vaulted spaces and bringing the incomparable Provençal springtime palette into the house: sunflowers, poppies, deep green cyprus trees and the shifting blues of the sky, are all reflected in the shades on the walls.

Michel Klein

Le styliste Michel Klein, qui dessine désormais les collections de haute couture de Guy Laroche, est reconnu partout dans le monde comme un moderniste dont les créations sobres et monochromes sont des exemples de pureté. En revanche, quand il s'agit de décorer sa maison, Klein croit en la couleur. Dans sa retraite provençale, près d'Arles, il a peint chaque pièce d'un ton différent, rivalisant de luminosité. Avec l'ivresse d'un enfant devant sa première boîte de couleurs, il a badigeonné les murs de fuchsia, de jaune canari, de rouge vif et de bleu vert qui changent de teintes au gré de la lumière. De fait, il avoue que la partie la plus excitante de la restauration de son mas a été de choisir les couleurs dans l'arc-en-ciel de pigments proposés par la boutique parisienne de Sennelier. Ce mélange audacieux a fait des miracles: toutes les couleurs du printemps provençal, tournesols, coquelicots, verts sombres des cyprès et bleus changeants du ciel se retrouvent sur les murs de la maison.

Der Modeschöpfer Michel Klein, der inzwischen die Kollektion für das Couture-Haus Guy Laroche entwirft, ist international als Modernist anerkannt. Seine monochromen, nüchternen Kollektionen sind oft Variationen von Schlichtheit. Im Gegensatz zu seinem Modeschaffen schätzt er jedoch bei Innenräumen starke Farben als dekoratives Element. In seinem provenzalischen Haus in der Nähe von Arles wählte er für jeden Raum einen anderen leuchtenden Farbton. Mit der Begeisterung eines Kindes, das aufgeregt vor einem Kasten mit Fingerfarben sitzt, entschied er sich bei der Renovierung seines »mas« für Fuchsie, Kanariengelb, Leuchtendrot, Smaragdgrün und ein Malvenblau, das sich je nach Lichteinfall verändert. Er gesteht sogar, der aufregendste Moment bei dem ganzen Projekt sei für ihn die Auswahl der Farben aus der Palette an Pigmenten gewesen, die bei Sennelier in Paris angeboten wurden. Die kühne Mischung hat sich optimal bewährt; sie macht die niedrigen, gewölbten Räume offener und bringt die einzigartige Palette der provenzalischen Frühlingsfarben ins Haus: Sonnenblumen, Mohn, tiefgrüne Zypressen und das changierende Blau des Himmels – all das spiegelt sich in den Wandfarben.

Above and right: the garden façade of the house with topiaries, aloes and geraniums and a combination of antique garden furniture.
On the following pages: A "star" chandelier by Orn Gudmundarsen lights a summer dinner table in the garden under the century-old plane trees.

Ci-dessus et à droite: la façade côté jardin avec ses buissons, ses aloès, ses géraniums et un ensemble de meubles de jardin anciens.
Double page suivante: un lustre «étoile» dessiné par Orn Gudmundarsen éclaire le dîner d'été sous les platanes centenaires.

Oben und rechts: Die Gartenseite des Hauses mit Formbäumen, Aloe und Geranien sowie einer Ansammlung alter Gartenmöbel.
Folgende Doppelseite: Der Stern-Kerzenleuchter von Orn Gudmundarsen beleuchtet im Garten einen Sommer-Eßtisch unter jahrhundertealten Platanen.

Facing page: *a bedroom with a bed which is an Empire "lit bateau".*
The red leatherette cupboard is a gypsy piece.
Above: *a corridor which is an unabashed celebration of contrasting*
colours with the rooms. The white wrought-iron chairs are 1940s.

Page de gauche: *une des chambres à coucher avec un lit bateau*
Empire et une commode de gitan en similicuir.
Ci-dessus: *le couloir qui, avec les chambres, est un hymne à la cou-*
leur. Les chaises blanches en fer forgé datent des années quarante.

Linke Seite: *ein Schlafzimmer. Das Bett ist ein »Lit bateau« aus der*
Empire-Zeit, das mit rotem Kunstleder überzogene Schränkchen eine
Zigeunerarbeit.
Oben: *Der Flur zeigt zusammen mit den Zimmern die unverhohlene*
Freude an Kontrastfarben. Die weißen schmiedeeisernen Stühle stam-
men aus den vierziger Jahren.

Above: The wooden Louis XVI bed is upholstered in Colombian ticking, the armchairs are 18th century, and the painting on the right is by Jacquemond.
Facing page: a view into the lilac-blue bedroom from the corridor, showing a Napoleon III chair and a gilt Restoration mirror.

Ci-dessus: le lit en bois Louis XVI est tapissé de toile à matelas colombienne. Les fauteuils sont du XVIIIe siècle et le tableau sur la droite est signé Jacquemond.
Page de droite: la chambre bleu lilas vue du couloir, avec une chaise Napoléon III et un miroir Restauration en bois doré.

Oben: Das hölzerne Louis-XVI.-Bett ist mit kolumbianischem Matratzendrillich gepolstert, die Lehnstühle sind aus dem 18. Jahrhundert, das Gemälde rechts ist von Jacquemond.
Rechte Seite: Blick vom Flur in das blauviolette Schlafzimmer mit einem Napoleon-III-Stuhl und einem Spiegel aus der Restaurationszeit.

Unang, which owes its Germanic-sounding name to the Visigoth occupation of Provence, lies quietly, almost secretly nestled against the hillside in the valley of the Nesque River. It is thought to be the oldest chateau in the Vaucluse; indeed a thousand years have passed since the first mention of the property was recorded, when Charles, King of Provence, donated it to the church. For many hundreds of years an important religious retreat, it is still flanked by the ancient private chapel dedicated to Saint Gabriel. The main building's present appearance owes more to a certain Augustin Raymond who embellished the exterior in the late 18th century and added the charming "jardin à la Française" in clipped box. Run as a private vineyard by a brother and sister team who occasionally rent out rooms, Unang slumbers, forgotten by time, and gazes out over a still unspoilt wooded valley.

Château Unang

Unang, qui doit son nom aux consonances germaniques à l'occupation de la Provence par les Wisigoths, est niché tranquillement, presque secrètement, dans les collines de la vallée du Nesque. On le tient pour le plus vieux château du Vaucluse: en effet, il est déjà mentionné dans des archives vieilles de mille ans, à l'occasion de son don à l'Eglise par Charles, roi de Provence. Importante retraite religieuse pendant de longs siècles, il est encore flanqué d'une ancienne chapelle privée dédiée à saint Gabriel. Le corps principal du bâtiment doit surtout son aspect actuel à un certain Augustin Raymond, qui en a embelli les façades à la fin du XVIIIe siècle et a ajouté un charmant jardin à la française en buis taillé. Aujourd'hui domaine vinicole géré par un frère et une sœur qui y louent parfois des chambres, Unang somnole, oublié par le temps, et contemple la vallée boisée encore intacte qui s'étend à ses pieds.

Der germanisch anmutende Name Unang erinnert daran, daß die Provence einst von den Westgoten besetzt war. Das Schloß liegt in ruhiger, fast abgeschiedener Lage an die Hänge des Tals des Nesque geschmiegt. Es gilt als das älteste Schloß des Vaucluse und wurde zum ersten Mal vor tausend Jahren erwähnt, als der provenzalische König Karl es der Kirche schenkte. Jahrhundertelang war Unang ein wichtiger religiöser Zufluchtsort, und noch heute grenzt das Schloß an eine alte Kapelle, die dem Erzengel Gabriel geweiht ist. Das jetzige Erscheinungsbild des Hauptgebäudes ist im wesentlichen auf einen gewissen Augustin Raymond zurückzuführen, der das Äußere gegen Ende des 18. Jahrhunderts verschönerte und den bezaubernden französischen Garten mit den präzise beschnittenen Buchsbaumfiguren anlegte. Das Schloß wird heute von einem Geschwisterpaar als privater Weingarten und gelegentlich auch als Hotel genutzt, schlummert jedoch ansonsten abseits vom Lauf der Zeit an seinem Aussichtspunkt hoch über dem noch unverdorbenen, waldreichen Tal.

On the previous pages: *a view of the well-kept garden which surrounds the chateau.*
Above: *a corner of the beamed salon.*
Facing page: *a welcoming fire in the hall. Successive owners have transformed the classical proportions of a medieval chateau into a labyrinth of small rooms. Only a few original features remain, and Unang's interior documents the repeated changes in use common to many of the older Provençal chateaux. They were first transformed from feudal fortresses into monasteries, then into pleasure pavilions in the 18th century, and eventually into private homes or farms during the last century.*

Double page précédente: *le jardin très bien entretenu qui entoure le château.*
Ci-dessus: *le salon avec ses poutres apparentes.*
Page de droite: *un feu crépite chaleureusement dans le hall. Les différents propriétaires qui se sont succédés ont modifié les proportions classiques du château médiéval, devenu un dédale de petites pièces. Il reste peu des traits originaux d'Unang qui illustre les nom-*

breux changements de fonction subis par la plupart des vieux châteaux provençaux. Ces forteresses médiévales furent d'abord transformées en monastères, puis en pavillons de plaisance au XVIIIe siècle et enfin en maisons particulières ou en domaines agricoles au cours du siècle passé.

Vorhergehende Doppelseite: *Blick über den gepflegen Garten, der das Schloß umgibt.*
Oben: *eine Ecke des von einer Balkendecke überspannten Salons.*
Rechte Seite: *In der Halle lodert ein einladendes Kaminfeuer. Mehrere Besitzer haben nacheinander die klassischen Proportionen des mittelalterlichen Schlosses in ein Labyrinth kleiner Räume verwandelt. Von den Originalelementen blieben nur wenige erhalten. Die Innenausstattung zeugt von der immer wieder veränderten Nutzung, der viele der alten provenzalischen Châteaux sich unterwerfen mußten, die zunächst von feudalen Festungen in Klöster, im 18. Jahrhundert dann in Lustschlösser und im letzten Jahrhundert schließlich in private Wohnhäuser oder Gutshöfe umfunktioniert wurden.*

There are many ways of living in Provence: this small "mas", situated near Vaison-la-Romaine, has been restored in a completely original manner by the designer and decorator Denis Colomb. An "Aixerois" by birth, Colomb has a true understanding of the intimate character of his native Provence, and in accordance with his clients' wishes, he has avoided the conventions usually applied when decorating local holiday homes. The countryside in this mountainous area of the Vaucluse can be particularly wild and the plant growth invasive. Denis has preserved the garden much as the previous country tenant, a "paysan", left it and only slightly tamed the invading creepers that have almost swallowed the house. Inside he has kept the roughness of the walls, the uneven floor and the generally shabby-chic atmosphere of the place. Indeed, the traces of his intervention have been kept to a minimum. His client is thrilled as his interpretation is close to her conception of what modern-day country living is all about.

Denis Colomb

On peut vivre la Provence de multiples façons: ce petit mas situé près de Vaison-la-Romaine a été restauré avec une grande originalité par le décorateur et designer Denis Colomb. Aixois de naissance, Colomb a une profonde connaissance du caractère intime de sa Provence natale et, tout en respectant les souhaits de ses clients, il a évité les conventions qui caractérisent les maisons de vacances de la région. Le paysage de cette région montagneuse du Vaucluse est particulièrement sauvage et la végétation, envahissante. Denis a conservé le jardin pratiquement tel que l'avait laissé son ancien propriétaire, un agriculteur, se contentant d'apprivoiser les plantes grimpantes qui avaient pratiquement englouti la maison. A l'intérieur, il a préservé la texture brute des murs, le sol irrégulier et l'atmosphère générale d'élégant délabrement. De fait, son intervention est restée minime. Sa cliente est aux anges, car son intérieur correspond exactement à l'idée qu'elle se faisait de la vie moderne à la campagne.

Man kann auf ganz unterschiedliche Weise in der Provence wohnen. Dieser kleine »mas« in der Nähe von Vaison-la-Romaine wurde vom Designer und Innenausstatter Denis Colomb vollkommen originalgetreu renoviert. Colomb wurde in Aix geboren und hat schon von daher viel Sinn für den geheimen Charakter seiner provenzalischen Heimat. Im Einklang mit den Wünschen seiner Kunden läßt er bei der Renovierung von Ferienhäusern die üblichen Konventionen außer acht. Die Landschaft in diesem gebirgigen Teil des Vaucluse ist zum Teil recht wild, und die Vegetation überwuchert fast alles. Denis bewahrte den Garten im wesentlichen so, wie ihn der Vorbesitzer, ein Bauer, hinterließ, und stutzte lediglich die enormen Kletterpflanzen, die das Haus fast zu verschlingen drohten. Im Innern behielt er die rauhen Wände, den unebenen Fußboden und die insgesamt schäbig-schicke Atmosphäre des Hauses im großen und ganzen bei und verwischte die Spuren seiner Eingriffe, so gut es ging. Seine Kundin ist begeistert von seiner Konzeption, die ihren eigenen Vorstellungen von einem modernen Landleben entspricht.

Provence Interiors   Xavier Nicod

This village house, perched high above the plain and sheltered by the Lubéron mountains, is an imposing 16th and 17th-century construction. The Mayers bought it many years ago from a military gentleman whose family had lived in the house for several generations. Tony Mayer, author of a book on "La Vie Anglaise", considers himself something of an Anglophile and is greatly amused by the hordes of English tourists who have taken to invading the quiet hilltop village during the summer months. Owing to the Mayers' advanced age, the house has remained untouched for the last twenty years and thus could be considered a rare example of a well-preserved interior in a style that has almost vanished. Many comparable gracious Provençal properties have been bought up by a new generation of aesthetes and been transformed.

Marie-Thérèse et Tony Mayer

Cette imposante bâtisse des XVIe et XVIIe siècles est située dans un village haut perché au-dessus de la plaine et abrité par les montagnes du Lubéron. Les Mayer l'ont achetée il y a de nombreuses années à un militaire dont la famille y vivait depuis plusieurs générations. Anglophile averti, Tony Mayer, auteur de «La vie anglaise», est très amusé par les nuées de touristes britanniques qui s'abattent sur la colline tranquille pendant les mois d'été. Du fait de l'âge avancé des Mayer, la maison n'a pas changé depuis vingt ans et constitue donc un exemple rare d'un style de décor comme on n'en voit plus. De nombreuses belles demeures provençales ont été rachetées depuis par une nouvelle génération d'esthètes qui ont imposé d'autres concepts de la décoration intérieure.

Das hoch über der Ebene im Schatten des Lubéron-Gebirges liegende Haus ist ein eindrucksvolles Gebäude aus dem 16. und 17. Jahrhundert. Die Mayers kauften es vor vielen Jahren einem Offizier ab, dessen Familie es mehrere Generationen lang bewohnt hatte. Tony Mayer, Autor eines Buches über »La Vie Anglaise«, hält sich selbst für ausgeprägt anglophil und amüsiert sich königlich über die Horden englischer Touristen, die in den Sommermonaten in das stille Bergdörfchen einfallen. Aufgrund des hohen Alters des Ehepaares ist an dem Haus in den letzten zwanzig Jahren nichts mehr verändert worden. Es besitzt daher eine gut erhaltene Innenausstattung in einem eigentlich nicht mehr üblichen Stil. Viele ähnlich schöne Besitzungen in der Provence sind mittlerweile von einer jungen Generation von Liebhabern aufgekauft und umgestaltet worden.

On the previous pages: *the view from the disused well in the garden, previously the only source of water in the house.*
Below: *the library, a witness to Tony Mayer's literary activities. In their youth, the Mayers belonged to a highly artistic circle and frequently visited personalities such as Cocteau and Picabia, both of whose drawings and other mementos are present in the room. In the foreground, rustic Provençal chairs and a solid, traditional dining-table now used as a desk.*

Double page précédente: *la vue depuis le puits condamné du jardin, autrefois la seule source d'eau de la maison.*
Ci-dessous: *la bibliothèque, siège des activités littéraires de Tony Mayer. Dans leur jeunesse, les Mayer faisaient partie de l'élite artistique et fréquentaient des personnalités telles que Cocteau et Picabia, dont des dessins et autres souvenirs ornent cette pièce. Au premier plan, des chaises rustiques provençales et une lourde table de salle à manger traditionnelle reconvertie en bureau.*

Vorhergehende Doppelseite: *der Blick in den Garten von dem stillgelegten Brunnen aus, der früher die einzige Wasserquelle des Hauses war.*
Unten: *Die Bibliothek bezeugt Tony Mayers reges literarisches Interesse. In ihrer Jugend waren die Mayer in bedeutenden Künstlerkreisen zu Hause und hatten Kontakt zu Persönlichkeiten wie Cocteau und Picabia, deren Zeichnungen und andere Werke im Raum zu sehen sind. Im Vordergrund rustikale provenzalische Stühle und ein solider altehrwürdiger Eßtisch, der heute als Schreibtisch dient.*

Above: The original 16th-century fireplace is the focal point of the long, low-beamed room. The ceiling has been painted white in order to give the room a greater volume. In the foreground, an 18th-century cane-bottomed bench, known as a "radassié", which is typically Provençal.
On the following pages: the "salon d'été" in what used to be the barn. The art nouveau pieces are by Jacques Majorelle.

Ci-dessus: Cette longue pièce au plafond bas et aux poutres apparentes est dominée par la cheminée d'origine qui date du XVIe siècle. Le plafond a été peint en blanc pour agrandir le volume. Au premier plan, un banc canné typiquement provençal, ou «radassié», qui date du XVIIIe siècle.
Double page suivante: le salon d'été dans l'ancienne grange. Les meubles Art nouveau sont de Jacques Majorelle.

Oben: Der originalgetreue Kamin aus dem 16. Jahrhundert ist das Herz des langgestreckten Raumes. Die niedrige Balkendecke wurde weiß gestrichen, um den Raum größer wirken zu lassen. Im Vordergrund eine typisch provenzalische Bank mit einer aus Schilf geflochtenen Sitzfläche, »Radassié« genannt.
Folgende Doppelseite: der »Salon d'été«, das Wohnzimmer für den Sommer, in der ehemaligen Scheune. Die Jugendstilstücke stammen von Jacques Majorelle.

Provence Interiors   Anna Bonde et Arne Tengblad

The Swedish painter Arne Tengblad discovered the Lubéron in 1963, while visiting a painter friend. He bought his first ruin for next to nothing, and with Anna Bonde decided to move to Provence for good. They have since bought and restored several houses: once they have made them comfortable, they tend to get the urge to move on and start again. Indeed, this partly troglodytic village house is their sixth. The house assumed its present appearance in the 1680s when a village girl was married off to the Spanish court of Asturias. While cleaning out the cellar Tengblad discovered a 12th-century coat of arms, proof of the building's mysterious past. Together the couple have tried to restore some of the original gracious feeling of space and have created an unexpected loft-like area for their main room. The house is decorated with market finds and fine pieces of Swedish furniture for which Anna designs the upholstery fabric.

Anna Bonde et
Arne Tengblad

Le peintre suédois Arne Tengblad a découvert le Lubéron en 1963 en rendant visite à un ami peintre. Il y a acheté sa première ruine pour une bouchée de pain et, avec Anna Bonde, a décidé de s'établir définitivement en Provence. Depuis, ils ont acheté et restauré plusieurs maisons: chaque fois, après les avoir rendues confortables, ils ont été pris d'une envie de déménager et de repartir à zéro. Cette maison de village en partie troglodyte est leur sixième. Elle n'a revêtu son aspect actuel que vers 1680, lorsqu'une jeune fille du village fut mariée à un ambassadeur de la cour du prince des Asturies. En nettoyant la cave, Tengblad a toutefois découvert aussi un blason du XIIe siècle, preuve du passé mystérieux de l'édifice. Le couple a tenté de retrouver certains des élégants volumes d'origine et a créé un espace inattendu de type loft qui leur sert de pièce principale. La maison est décorée de trouvailles dénichées sur le marché local et de beaux meubles suédois pour lesquels Anna dessine des tissus.

Der schwedische Maler Arne Tengblad lernte den Lubéron 1963 kennen, als er dort einen befreundeten Maler besuchte. Seine erste Ruine bekam er fast geschenkt, worauf er beschloß, zusammen mit Anna Bonde für immer in die Provence zu ziehen. Seither haben die beiden mehrere Häuser gekauft und restauriert. Sobald sie ein Haus fertig eingerichtet haben, drängt es sie schon, mit dem nächsten wieder von vorne zu beginnen. Das hier abgebildete Haus, das zum Teil wie eine Höhle wirkt, ist ihr sechstes. Das Gebäude erhielt sein heutiges Aussehen in den achtziger Jahren des 17. Jahrhunderts, als ein Mädchen einen Gesandten vom Hofe des Prinzen von Asturien heiratete. Beim Entrümpeln des Kellers fand Tengblad auch ein Wappen aus dem 12. Jahrhundert, das von der geheimnisvollen Geschichte des Hauses zeugt. Gemeinsam bemühte sich das Paar, einige der noch originalen schönen Räume zu restaurieren, und richtete eine ungewöhnliche, dachhohe Halle als Hauptraum ein. Die Einrichtung besteht aus Zufallsfunden und aparten schwedischen Antiquitäten, für die Anna selbst die Polsterstoffe entwirft.

Above: A school teaching aid picturing a zebra hangs above a simple day bed in wrought iron designed by Anna. The iron chair was found in a market.
Detail right: a Swedish chair and a baroque Italian 17th-century chandelier.
Facing page: The main room houses a collection of contemporary art.

Ci-dessus: une planche d'école représentant un zèbre est suspendue au-dessus d'un simple lit de repos en fer forgé dessiné par Anna. La chaise en métal a été trouvée sur le marché.
Détail de droite: une chaise suédoise et un lustre baroque italien du XVIIe siècle.
Page de droite: la collection d'art contemporain dans la pièce principale.

Oben: Ein Schulhilfsmittel mit einem Zebra hängt über einer von Anna selbst entworfenen, schlichten schmiedeeisernen Liege. Der Eisenstuhl wurde auf einem Markt entdeckt.
Detail rechts: ein schwedischer Sessel und ein barocker italienischen Kerzenleuchter aus dem 17. Jahrhundert.
Rechte Seite: Der Hauptraum beherbergt eine Sammlung moderner Kunst.

Niched deep in the stone of a hilltop village in the Lubéron, Nicole de Vesian's home is a completely original creation. As soon as you step through the door, the intoxicating smell of lavender leaves you light-headed. Underfoot, in the entrance, are loose, large pebbles, known as "galets", from the nearby river, the Durance. The house, issue of the stone itself, was converted from two ruined cottages and the covered lane that ran between them. Three steps up to the guest room, three steps down to the lounge, it is oddly distributed and betrays its unusual origins. Everywhere the monochromatic beige, cream and off-white, beloved of Nicole, allow the strong contours of the stone to impose a very particular atmosphere. The difference between the garden and its pebbled paths and the stone-walled interior with its bouquets of dried flowers and budding plants seems minimal.

Nicole de Vesian

Profondément nichée dans la pierre d'un village haut perché du Lubéron, la maison de Nicole de Vesian est une création très originale. Dès que l'on passe la porte, on est saisi par le parfum enivrant de la lavande. Le sol du vestibule est pavé de gros galets qui proviennent de la Durance voisine. La maison, née de la pierre elle-même, a été construite en réunissant deux bâtisses en ruines et l'allée couverte qui les reliait. On monte trois marches pour accéder à la chambre d'amis, on en descend trois pour se rendre au salon: la distribution déroutante des pièces témoigne des origines inhabituelles de la maison. Partout, les tons mono-chromes de beige, de crème et de blanc cassé, chers à Nicole, lais-sent la pierre nue imposer une atmosphère très particulière. Entre le jardin et ses allées de gravier, et l'intérieur avec ses murs en pierres brutes, ses bouquets de fleurs séchées et ses plantes vertes, la frontière est ténue.

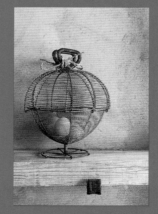

Tief in den Fels eines Bergdorfes im Lubéron gegraben liegt Nicole de Vesians ausgesprochen originelles Haus. Sobald man durch die Tür tritt, steigt einem der berauschende Lavendelduft zu Kopfe. Der Fuß-bodenbelag im Eingangsgereich besteht aus großen, losen Kieselstei-nen, »galets«, die vom Ufer der nahe gelegenen Durance stammen. Das Haus ist teils direkt in den Fels hineingebaut, teils aus zwei verfallenen Bauernhäusern und dem überdachten Pfad zwischen ih-nen zusammengesetzt. Drei Stufen führen hinauf zum Gästezimmer, drei Stufen hinab zum Wohnzimmer – mit seiner eigenwilligen Aufteilung verrät das Haus seine besonderen Ursprünge. Die von Ni-cole geliebten, monochrom eingesetzten Töne Beige, Creme und ge-brochen Weiß, die die kraftvollen Konturen des Steins unterstreichen, verleihen dem Anwesen eine ganz eigentümliche Atmosphäre. Zwischen dem Garten mit seinem Kiesweg und den Innenräumen mit den Steinwänden, Trockenblumensträußen und üppigen Topf-pflanzen besteht nur ein minimaler Unterschied.

On the previous pages: a view of Nicole de Vesian's innovative garden that has been a source of inspiration for many. By concentrating on hardy local varieties, as opposed to more showy imported plants, she has refined the concept of the Provençal garden. A hundred shades of green and grey, the indigenous aromatics clipped into spheres, and the proud and long-living trees of the area give a distinction and strange beauty to Nicole's terraced "terrain". Her creation is not about superfluous decoration, or about flowers even, but about form, and echoing the true shapes and colours of the region.
On these pages: the simple kitchen which makes a virtue of its clean lines and functional wooden furnishings.
On the following pages: the salon.

Double page précédente: le jardin de Nicole de Vesian dont beaucoup se sont inspirés. En préférant les variétés robustes de la région aux plantes plus spectaculaires venues d'ailleurs, elle a affiné le concept du jardin provençal. Une palette très nuancée de verts et de gris, des plantes aromatiques locales taillées en boules et les vieux arbres fiers de la région donnent à ce terrain en terrasse une distinction et une beauté étrange. Nicole de Vesian ne s'embarrasse pas de détails décoratifs superflus, ni même de fleurs, mais se concentre avant tout sur une vision d'ensemble qui rappelle les vraies formes et couleurs de la région.
Page de gauche et ci-dessus: le décor simple de la cuisine qui met en valeur ses lignes sobres et ses meubles en bois fonctionnels.
Double page suivante: le salon.

Vorhergehende Doppelseite: Ansichten von Nicoles innovativem Garten, der einen starken Einfluß auf andere Anlagen ausgeübt hat. Durch die Konzentration auf widerstandsfähige regionale Gewächse anstelle spektakulärer, importierter Pflanzen verfeinerte Nicole das Konzept des provenzalischen Gartens. Grün und Grau in Hunderten von Nuancen, zu Kugeln geschnittene einheimische Aromaten und die stolzen, langlebigen Bäume der Region verleihen dem terrassenförmig angelegten Garten eine ganz eigene, fremdartige Schönheit. Ihr geht es nicht um überflüssige Dekors, nicht einmal um Blumen, sondern allein um Formen. Der Garten spiegelt die Konturen und Farben, die in dieser Region tatsächlich zu finden sind.
Diese Doppelseite: Die schlichte Küche profitiert optisch von klaren Linien und funktionalen Holzmöbeln.
Folgende Doppelseite: der Salon.

Above and facing page: the bathroom and a little stone sink for rinsing one's hands.
On the following pages: the partly troglodytic summer dining-room which gives onto the garden through big double doors. Nicole's favourite room, it overflows with glorious clutter: garden utensils, straw hats and baskets, cuttings being carefully nurtured, garden furniture and dried flowers.

Ci-dessus et page de droite: la salle de bains et un petit lavabo en pierre pour se laver les mains.
Double page suivante: la salle à manger d'été à demi-creusée dans la roche donne sur le jardin à travers deux grandes double portes. Pièce préférée de Nicole, elle regorge d'un pittoresque bric-à-brac: outils de jardinage, chapeaux de paille, paniers en osier, boutures soigneusement nourries, meubles de jardin et fleurs séchées.

Oben und rechte Seite: das Badezimmer und ein kleines steinernes Becken zum Händewaschen.
Folgende Doppelseite: die teilweise höhlenartige Sommerküche, deren große Flügeltür zum Garten hinausgeht. Nicoles Lieblingsraum enthält ein prachtvolles Sammelsurium von Gartengeräten, Strohhüten und Körben, liebevoll gezogenen Ablegern, Gartenmöbeln und Trockenblumen.

Built on the site of a Celtic "oppidum", the Château d'Ansouis, fiefdom and home of the Duc de Sabran-Pontevès, towers over the pretty stone Provençal village of the same name. Partly open to the public but still the family home of the Duc and Duchesse and their four children, it gives an excellent idea of what a grand house is really like to live in. However unlikely it may seem, this huge rabbit warren of a house really has managed to conserve a cosy atmosphere. This could be due to the fact that, apart from a short period after the Revolution, the Sabrans have been living here for the last seven hundred years. Originally a 12th and 14th-century fortress, Ansouis was beautified in the 17th century. This later addition represents the main body of the chateau but the interior is a real "gruyère", to quote the Duke.

Château d'Ansouis

Bâti sur le site d'une ancienne citadelle celte, le Château d'Ansouis, fief et demeure du duc de Sabran-Pontevès, surplombe le ravissant village provençal du même nom. Partiellement ouvert au public, il est toujours habité par le duc, la duchesse et leurs quatre enfants, ce qui donne aux visiteurs une excellente idée de ce que signifie «la vie de château». Contre toute attente, une atmosphère douillette baigne ce gigantesque dédale de pièces et de couloirs. Cela s'explique sans doute par le fait qu'à l'exception d'une brève période après la Révolution, les Sabran y vivent depuis sept siècles. A l'origine forteresse des XIIe et XIVe siècles, le corps principal du château a été rénové et embelli au XVIIe. En revanche, nous confie le duc, l'intérieur est un «véritable gruyère».

Das über einem keltischen »oppidum« erbaute Schloß Ansouis, Lehen und zugleich Wohnsitz der Herzöge von Sabran-Pontevès, blickt auf das hübsche provenzalische Dorf gleichen Namens hinab. Das Schloß, in dem noch heute der Herzog mit seiner Frau und seinen vier Kindern lebt und das teilweise zur Besichtigung freigegeben ist, gibt einen vorzüglichen Eindruck davon, was es bedeutet, in einem echten Herrenhaus zu wohnen. Und so unwahrscheinlich es auch klingen mag, dieses Schloß, das aus einem ungeheuren Wirrwarr verschachtelter Räume besteht, hat sich eine gemütliche Atmosphäre bewahrt. Vielleicht liegt es daran, daß die Familie Sabran mit nur einer kurzen Unterbrechung nach der französischen Revolution seit siebenhundert Jahren hier lebt. Das im 12. und 14. Jahrhundert ursprünglich als Festung angelegte Schloß wurde im 17. Jahrhundert umgebaut. Der jüngere, regelmäßigere Bauteil stellt heute das Hauptgebäude der Anlage dar, das Innere jedoch ist, um den Hausherrn zu zitieren, ein regelrechter Irrgarten.

Page 174: *a view of the splendid avenue of cypresses that lead off from the main gate. The famous hanging gardens at Ansouis include a topiary maze in clipped box, and the view from the terraces of the rolling Provençal counryside is quite breathtaking, as can be seen on the previous pages.*
Above: *one of the historical 17th-century bedrooms. Many of these are furnished with family heirlooms inherited from "tante" Huberte and "tante" Gersende, who were, respectively, the last Marquise of Sabran-Pontevès and the Marquise des Isnards.*
Facing page: *the games room in the present Duchess' private apartments with its fancy plasterwork and pistacho paintwork.*
On the following pages: *the vaulted kitchen, one of the oldest rooms in the chateau, that dates from the times of the popular Provençal Saints Elzéar and Delphine de Sabran, whose lives were played out in the corridors of Ansouis.*

Page 174: *la majestueuse allée de cyprès qui mène au château. Les fameux jardins suspendus d'Ansouis comprennent un labyrinthe en buis taillés. Depuis les terrasses, on a une vue à couper le souffle sur les douces collines provençales, comme on peut le constater sur la double page précédente.*
Ci-dessus: *l'une des chambres historiques, avec son décor du XVIIe siècle. La plupart contiennent des meubles de famille hérités de «tante» Huberte et «tante» Gersende qui furent respectivement, la dernière marquise de Sabran-Pontevès et la marquise des Isnards.*
Page de droite: *la salle de jeu des appartements privés de la duchesse actuelle, avec ses murs pistache et ses «pâtisseries».*
Double page suivante: *la cuisine voûtée, l'une des pièces les plus anciennes du château. Elle remonte aux temps d'Elzéar et de Delphine de Sabran, deux saints provençaux très populaires qui vécurent à Ansouis.*

Page 174: *ein Blick in die prachtvolle Zypressenallee, die vom Haupttor zum Haus führt. Zu den berühmten hängenden Gärten von Ansouis gehört ein Labyrinth aus kunstvoll beschnittenem Buchsbaum. Die Aussicht von den Terrassen auf die provenzalische Hügellandschaft ist einzigartig, wie die vorhergehende Doppelseite beweist.*
Oben: *eines der originalgetreuen Schlafzimmer aus dem 17. Jahrhundert. Viele davon sind mit Möbeln aus Familienbesitz eingerichtet, Erbstücke von »Tante« Huberte, der letzten Marquise de Sabran-Pontevès, und »Tante« Gersende, der Marquise des Isnards.*
Rechte Seite: *Zu den Privatgemächern der jetzigen Herzogin gehört dieser Salon mit seinen »Pâtisseries« aus Stuck und den pistaziengrün gestrichenen Wänden.*
Folgende Doppelseite: *Die mit einer Gewölbedecke ausgestattete Küche ist einer der ältesten Räume des Schlosses und stammt noch aus der Epoche der bis heute verehrten provenzalischen Heiligen Elzéar und Delphine de Sabran, die hier in Ansouis lebten und wirkten.*

On the previous pages: *the view from the house over lavender fields.*
Above: *Vial's study adjacent to his bedroom and hidden partly underground in the discreet extension cleverly built so that it cannot be perceived from ground level. The bookcase originally belonged to Montpellier University and the framed pictures are reproductions of Leonardo da Vinci's drawings. The screen is an 18th-century "chinoiserie", such as the one in the bedroom on the top of the facing page.*

Double page précédente: *les champs de lavande vus de la maison.*
Ci-dessus: *le bureau de Vial, attenant à sa chambre. Il est partiellement enterré grâce à une extension discrète et astucieuse du bâtiment, invisible de l'extérieur. La bibliothèque appartenait autrefois à l'université de Montpellier et les dessins au mur sont des reproductions d'esquisses de Léonard de Vinci. Le paravent est une chinoiserie du XVIIIe siècle, tout comme celui de la chambre à la page de droite.*

Vorhergehende Doppelseite: *Blick vom Haus aus über Lavendelfelder.*
Oben: *Vials Arbeitsraum neben seinem Schlafzimmer ist teilweise unter der Erde in einem diskreten Anbau untergebracht, der so geschickt angelegt ist, daß man ihn vom Erdgeschoß aus nicht sieht. Der Bücherschrank stand einst in der Universität von Montpellier, die gerahmten Bilder sind Reproduktionen von Zeichnungen Leonardo da Vincis. Der Wandschirm ist eine Chinoiserie-Arbeit aus dem 18. Jahrhundert, ebenso wie das Pendant in dem auf der rechten Seite oben abgebildeten Schlafzimmer.*

Right: the denim-trimmed four-poster in the guest bedroom.
Below: the kitchen, which features a sofa and armchairs draped in white linen in order not to detract from the splendid architecture of the priory.

A droite: le lit à baldaquin de la chambre d'amis, avec sa passementerie en jean.
Ci-dessous: la cuisine, avec un canapé et des fauteuils tapissés de lin blanc afin que l'œil ne soit pas distrait de la magnifique architecture du prieuré.

Rechts: das mit Jeansstoff besetzte Himmelbett im Gästezimmer.
Unten: die Küche. Sofa und Lehnstühle sind mit weißem Leinen bezogen, damit nichts von der herrlichen Architektur der Abtei ablenkt.

This modern house designed by the architect Nasrine Faghih lies in
30 hectares of grounds in one of the most unspoilt parts of Provence.
Between Apt and Forcalquier, on the way to Jean Giono's beloved
highlands, on a site well protected from the mistral, the house is a
haven of peace with a splendid view of the Lubéron. It has been conceived as a modernistic interpretation of a "bastide", a country house,
incorporating certain Islamic precepts relative to the presence of
water and the role of the home as a refuge from the outer world. The
two swimming pools provide the illusion of an unbroken sheet of
water linking the inside and out: The strong light that floods the
minimalist interior is an integral element of the design, and the
acoustics and disposal of the rooms all obey ancient rules that make
for harmony. The illustration on the facing page shows a Martin
Szekely table on the terrace.

Nasrine Faghih

Cette bâtisse moderne dessinée par l'architecte Nasrine Faghih se
dresse sur un terrain de trente hectares situé entre Apt et Forcalquier, dans un des coins les mieux préservés de Provence. A l'abri
du mistral, sur la route qui mène aux hautes terres chères à Jean
Giono, c'est un havre de paix avec une vue splendide sur le Lubéron. Nasrine Faghih l'a conçue comme une bastide moderne, y in-
tégrant certains principes islamiques liés à la présence de l'eau et
au rôle de la maison comme refuge contre le monde extérieur. Les
deux piscines donnent l'illusion d'un plan d'eau ininterrompu re-
liant l'intérieur et l'extérieur. La lumière qui inonde l'intérieur mini-
maliste est partie intégrante du décor et les pièces ont été créées
selon des lois traditionnelles qui engendrent une atmosphère
d'harmonie. L'illustration à la page de droite montre une table de
Martin Szekely sur la terrasse.

Das von der Architektin Nasrine Faghih entworfene moderne Haus
steht auf einem 30 Hektar großen Grundstück in einer der schönsten
Gegenden der Provence. Zwischen Apt und Forcalquier, auf dem Weg
zu dem von Jean Giono so verehrten Hochland, liegt das Gebäude in
einer vor dem Mistral gut geschützten Stelle, wie ein Hort des Frie-
dens mit prachtvoller Aussicht auf den Lubéron. Angelegt wurde das
Haus als modernistische Form der »bastide«, wobei auch bestimmte
islamische Prinzipien berücksichtigt wurden, etwa was die Bedeutung
des Wassers und die Rolle des Heims als Ort des Rückzugs vor der
Welt angeht. Die beiden Swimmingpools wecken die Illusion einer
durchgehenden Wasserfläche, ohne Trennung zwischen innen und
außen. Das harte Licht, das auf die minimalistische Einrichtung fällt,
ist integraler Bestandteil des Designs. Akustik und Raumaufteilung
folgen uralten Regeln der Harmonie. Die Abbildung auf der rechten
Seite zeigt einen Tisch von Martin Szekely auf der Terrasse.

On the previous pages: a view of the inside swimming pool showing the sliding doors in metal and glass that connect the two pools.
Facing page: the bedroom with its narrow windows that look out onto a wooded slope, celebrated as being a great truffle-hunting ground.
Above: the living room that expresses the art of living simply surrounded by the minimum of possessions. The alcoves were designed specifically to house an impressive collection of paintings by Picasso.

Double page précédente: la piscine intérieure avec ses portes coulissantes à structure métallique qui s'ouvrent sur la piscine extérieure.
Page de gauche: la chambre à coucher avec ses fenêtres étroites qui donnent sur une colline boisée, connue pour être un excellent terrain truffier.
Ci-dessus: le salon, qui exprime l'art de vivre dans le dépouillement. Les alcôves ont été dessinées spécialement pour accueillir une impressionnante collection de tableaux de Picasso.

Vorhergehende Doppelseite: Blick über den Swimmingpool im Inneren des Hauses auf die Schiebetüren aus Metall und Glas, die beide Becken verbinden.
Linke Seite: Das Schlafzimmer mit den hohen, schmalen Fenstern blickt auf einen bewaldeten Hang, der als hervorragendes Trüffelgebiet gilt.
Oben: Das Wohnzimmer ist Ausdruck einer nur mit einem Minimum an Besitztümern auskommenden Lebenskunst. Die Nischen wurden eigens für die überragende Sammlung von Picasso-Gemälden konzipiert.

This troglodyte home, partly built in the living rock, is niched among the village Saignon's ancient foundations. Rosario Moreno and Aldo Franceschini arrived in 1964, via her native Argentina and Paris. A stone which happened to fall near the little square indicated that there might be a structure underneath a pile of ruins. In the excitement of the discovery, the land was bought for 500 francs, and the work on the house began. The young couple were penniless, to the point of not even being able to buy a proper spade. All the restoration and building work was done with improvised tools and a temperamental old Renault. They slowly managed to restore what turned out to be two giant vaulted cellars and eventually succeeded, with difficulty, in buying up the neighbouring ruins and restore them, acquiring enough space for a painter's studio, a terrace and a garden. It took them, with the help of Aldo's son, the best part of thirty years.

Rosario Moreno et Aldo Franceschini

Cette maison troglodyte, partiellement creusée dans le rocher, est nichée dans les anciennes fondations du village de Saignon. Rosario Moreno et Aldo Franceschini sont arrivés à Saignon en 1964, via l'Argentine et Paris. Une pierre, tombée accidentellement près de la petite place, leur a laissé deviner la présence d'une structure sous un tas de ruines. Excités par la perspective d'une découverte, ils achetèrent le terrain pour 500 francs et se mirent aussitôt à la tâche. Le jeune couple sans le sou n'avait pas même de quoi s'offrir une pelle digne de ce nom. Ils réalisèrent tous les travaux de restauration et de maçonnerie avec des outils de fortune et une vieille Renault caractérielle. Peu à peu, ils dégagèrent deux immenses caves voûtées. Ils parvinrent, non sans mal, a racheter les ruines adjacentes et à les restaurer, obtenant ainsi suffisamment d'espace pour créer un atelier de peintre, une terrasse et un jardin. Avec l'aide du fils d'Aldo, cela leur a demandé près de trente ans.

Dieses höhlenartige Haus, das zum Teil direkt in den Felsen hineingebaut wurde, liegt inmitten der alten Fundamente des Dorfes Saignon. Rosario Moreno und Aldo Franceschini kamen 1964 aus Argentinien und Paris hierher. Ein Stein, der an dem kleinen Dorfplatz zufällig herunterfiel, deutete darauf hin, daß sich unter einem Schutthaufen möglicherweise ein Gebäude verbarg. Begeistert von dem Fund kauften sie das Grundstück für 500 Francs und machten sich an die Arbeit. Das junge Paar besaß keinen Sou und konnte sich nicht einmal einen vernünftigen Spaten leisten. Die gesamten Instandsetzungs- und Bauarbeiten wurden mit improvisiertem Werkzeug und einem alten Renault vollbracht. Allmählich gelang es ihnen, zwei riesige Kellerräume mit Gewölben wiederherzustellen. Zu guter Letzt kauften sie unter großen Schwierigkeiten auch die angrenzenden Ruinen auf und restaurierten sie ebenfalls, so daß nun Platz für ein Atelier, eine Terrasse und einen Garten vorhanden ist. Alles in allem kostete sie das ganze Projekt fast dreißig Jahre.

On these pages: *Rosario Moreno's studio. These magestically proportioned stone cellars are probably the oldest structures in the village. Although Rosario Moreno bought the land and the ruins from a total of eight different owners in eight separate deals over fifteen or so years, it is believed that they could have all been part of the same property originally. Rosario Moreno was something of a trail blazer for the many artists who were to flock to the Lubéron in the seventies, many of whom encountered the same resistance as she did when she first decided to settle there.*
On the following pages: *the kitchen.*

Page de gauche, ci-dessus et ci-dessous: *l'atelier de Rosario Moreno. Ces caves en pierres aux proportions majestueuses sont sans doute les plus anciennes structures du village. Bien que Rosario Moreno ait racheté les terres et les ruines de huit propriétaires différents sur une période d'une quinzaine d'années, ces dernières pourraient autrefois avoir fait partie d'une même propriété. Rosario fait figure de pionnière pour les nombreux artistes qui ont envahi le Lubéron dans les années soixante-dix. La plupart se sont heurtés aux mêmes obstacles qu'elle lorsqu'elle a décidé de s'installer dans le village.*
Double page suivante: *la cuisine.*

Diese Doppelseite: *Rosario Morenos Atelier. Die majestätisch proportionierten Kellergewölbe dürften die ältesten Bauteile des Dorfes sein. Auch wenn Rosario Moreno Grundstück und Ruinen von insgesamt acht Eigentümern zusammenkaufte, wofür acht einzelne Kaufverträge und rund fünfzehn Jahre erforderlich waren, geht man davon aus, daß alles ursprünglich zu einem einzigen Besitz gehörte. Rosario Moreno bereitete in gewisser Weise den Weg für viele Künstler, die es in den siebziger Jahren in den Lubéron zog, wenn auch viele von ihnen mit den gleichen Widerständen zu kämpfen hatten wie sie selbst, als sie beschloß, sich hier niederzulassen.*
Folgende Doppelseite: *die Küche.*

The Rocchias come close to living the rural idyll that foreigners imagine when they dream of Provence. Sheltered by Cézanne's beloved mountain, the Mont Sainte-Victoire (see pp. 208/209) their little cabin overflows with the produce of the countryside. Jean-Marie is Provence's truffle expert, author of a popular book on the subject of the "black diamond", as he refers to it. He is also the proud owner of a very large, very greedy and inordinately friendly truffle pig, which has rather taken over the garden. She — for the 200-kilo gourmet is a she — has to share a pen with a gaggle of geese who were originally introduced with the aim of producing "foie gras"; these became awfully friendly with the family and thus were spared a fate worse than death. If Jean-Marie has been truffle hunting since the age of seven, his wife has been keeping bees for 16 years. She decants the delicately scented honey from her 120 hives which are placed in what has to be one of the least frequented but most breathtaking beauty spots in the region, with a perfect view of the Mont Sainte-Victoire.

Jean-Marie et Jennifer Rocchia

La vie des Rocchia ressemble un peu à ce rêve bucolique que font les étrangers quand ils pensent à la Provence. A l'abri de la montagne Sainte-Victoire chère à Cézanne (voir pp. 208/209), leur petit cabanon regorge des produits de la nature. Jean-Marie est l'expert en truffes de la Provence, auteur d'un livre sur «le diamant noir», comme il l'appelle. Il est également l'heureux propriétaire d'une énorme truie, très gloutonne et fort sympathique, qui règne en maîtresse sur le jardin. Cette gourmande de 200 kg partage toutefois ses quartiers avec un troupeau d'oies. A l'origine, ces dernières étaient destinées à finir en foie gras, mais elles ont témoigné tant d'affection à la famille qu'on leur a épargné cette mort cruelle. Si Jean-Marie chasse la truffe depuis l'âge de sept ans, sa femme élève des abeilles depuis 16 ans. Elle draine un miel au parfum délicat de ses 120 ruches dans un des plus beaux décors naturels de Provence, avec sa vue idéale sur la fameuse montagne.

Das Leben der Rocchias kommt der bäuerlichen Idylle, von der Ausländer beim Gedanken an die Provence träumen, sehr nahe. Im Schutze der von Cézanne geliebten Montagne Sainte-Victoire (s. S. 208/209) quillt ihr Häuschen fast über von den landwirtschaftlichen Produkten der Region. Jean-Marie ist der Trüffelexperte der Provence und Autor eines populären Buches über den »schwarzen Diamanten«, wie er die Trüffel nennt. Außerdem ist er stolzer Besitzer eines sehr großen, sehr freßgierigen und ausgesprochen freundlichen Trüffelschweins, das den Garten mehr oder weniger in Beschlag genommen hat. Sie — es handelt sich nämlich genaugenommen um eine Trüffelsau — muß ihren Koben mit einer Schar Gänse teilen, die ursprünglich für die Produktion von Gänsestopfleber angeschafft wurden, bis sich zwischen ihnen und der Familie eine wahre Freundschaft entwickelte und man ihnen ihr schreckliches Schicksal ersparte. Während Jean-Marie seit seinem siebten Lebensjahr Trüffel sammelt, ist seine Frau seit 16 Jahren Imkerin. Sie bereitet den zart duftenden Honig ihrer 120 Bienenvölker auf, die in einer der am wenigsten bekannten, dafür aber landschaftlich schönsten Ecken der Region mit wundervoller Aussicht auf die Montagne Sainte-Victoire stehen.

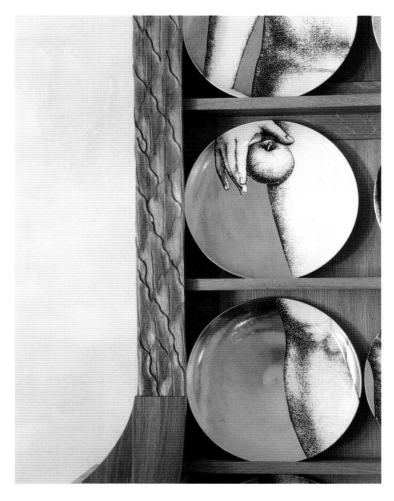

Above: *a detail of the inlaid sideboard, with its "organic" carvings. The figures are partly allegorical creations of Mathieu and Ray.*
Facing page, clockwise from top left: *an 18th-century carving above the piano in the living room; a dolphin motif on the carpet; damask curtains by Rubelli; the leaf motif, often repeated throughout the house.*

Ci-dessus: *un détail du buffet marqueté, dont les motifs représentent des formes anthropomorphes dessinées par Mathieu et Ray.*
Page de droite, en haut à gauche: *un bois sculpté du XVIIIe siècle au-dessus du piano du salon; puis dans le sens des aiguilles d'une montre: un motif du tapis représentant un dauphin; des rideaux damassés de chez Rubelli; un motif de feuille, que l'on retrouve partout dans la maison.*

Oben: *Ausschnitt aus der mit Einlegearbeiten versehenen Anrichte, die »organische« Schnitzereien aufweist. Die Figuren sind zum Teil allegorische Kreationen von Mathieu und Ray.*
Rechte Seite, im Uhrzeigersinn von oben links: *eine Schnitzarbeit aus dem 18. Jahrhundert über dem Flügel im Wohnzimmer; das Delphinmotiv des Teppichs; Damastvorhänge von Rubelli; das Blatt-motiv, das sich im ganzen Haus mehrfach wiederholt.*

Facing page: one of the pair of inlaid maple-wood desks in the bedroom of the Hadidas' two youngest daughters.
Above: an overall view of their bedroom, with a forties' mirrored chest of drawers and an original lighting fixture bought at L'Isle-sur-la-Sorgue. The smaller ones on either side of the beds were specially made to reproduce the design.

Page de gauche: un des deux bureaux en érable marqueté de la chambre des deux benjamines Hadida.
Ci-dessus: une vue générale de la chambre, avec une commode à trumeau des années quarante et des appliques originales chinées à L'Isle-sur-la-Sorgue. Des copies plus petites de ces dernières ont été placées de part et d'autre des lits.

Linke Seite: einer der beiden Ahornschreibtische mit Einlegearbeiten im Schlafzimmer der beiden jüngsten Hadida-Töchter.
Oben: Gesamtansicht ihres Schlafzimmers mit einer Spiegelkommode aus den vierziger Jahren und einer originellen Lampe, die in L'Isle-sur-la-Sorgue gekauft wurde. Die kleineren Lampen auf beiden Seiten der Betten wurden eigens als passende Pendants angefertigt.

Above: *the kitchen which looks as if it has been there for ever but in fact was entirely re-designed: doors were moved, the floor was laid, and the ceiling was raised.*
Facing page, clockwise from top left: *details of the wooden kitchen fittings carved with the text of a poem by Mistral; little glass vases by Bořek Šípek; the chicken wire on the doors; the lid of the elegant waste-disposal chute; a carved olive branch.*

Ci-dessus: *la cuisine, entièrement redécorée même si elle semble avoir toujours été ainsi: les portes ont été déplacées, le sol a été refait et le plafond rehaussé.*
Page de droite, en haut à gauche: *un détail des tiroirs du buffet sur lesquels est gravé un poème de Frédéric Mistral; puis dans le sens des aiguilles d'une montre: des petits vases en verre de Bořek Šípek; le grillage à poule des portes du buffet; le couvercle de l'élégant vide-ordures; une branche d'olivier sculptée.*

Oben: *Die Küche wirkt so, als habe sie nie anders ausgesehen, wurde jedoch in Wirklichkeit völlig neu konzipiert. Dafür wurden Türen versetzt, die Bodenfliesen gelegt und die Decke erhöht.*
Rechte Seite, im Uhrzeigersinn von oben links: *Details der hölzernen Kücheneinrichtung, in die der Text eines Gedichtes von Mistral geschnitzt ist; kleine Glasvasen von Bořek Šípek; die mit Maschendraht versehenen Schranktüren; der Deckel des eleganten Müllschluckers; ein geschnitzter Olivenzweig.*

While house-hunting in Provence, Lillian Williams and her husband
spotted this 17th-century pavilion. They were looking to buy a "hotel
particulier" in Aix in order to display Lillian's extensive costume
collection. Costumes, notably those of the 18th century, are Lillian's
passion and she has lent pieces for her collection to several museums
including the Metropolitan. Smitten by the gracious proportions, the
charming steps framing the garden façade, and the classically appointed "jardin à l'italienne", complete with fountains and terraces,
they acquired the property and Lillian set about transforming it into
the perfect, 18th-century "folie". Her taste for the theatrical is here
translated in a Baroque interior, where dressed mannequins are displayed in order to evoke Provençal life two hundred years ago. It is
this fascination with the daily occurrences, the small details of the
"quotidien" (on which she is writing a book), that distinguishes
Lillian's collection and gives it a particular vitality.

Lillian Williams

Lillian Williams et son mari ont découvert ce pavillon du XVIIe
siècle tandis qu'ils cherchaient un hôtel particulier à Aix pour accueillir la vaste collection de costumes de Lillian. Les costumes,
notamment ceux du XVIIIe siècle, sont la passion de Lillian qui a
prêté certaines de ses pièces à plusieurs musées, dont le Metropolitan de New York. Séduits par les proportions gracieuses du bâtiment, la charmante «descente d'escalier» de la façade côté jardin
et le jardin classique à l'italienne, avec son assortiment de terrasses et de fontaines, les Williams ont acheté la propriété, que Lillian s'est aussitôt mise à transformer en parfaite «folie» du XVIIIe
siècle. Son goût pour le théâtral s'est traduit ici par un décor baroque, dans lequel des mannequins habillés font revivre la Provence d'il y a deux cents ans. C'est cette fascination pour la vie de
l'époque, les petits détails du quotidien (sur lesquels elle est en
train d'écrire un livre), qui font de la collection de Lillian quelque
chose d'aussi vivant.

Auf der Suche nach einem Haus in der Provence entdeckten Lillian
Williams und ihr Mann dieses Schlößchen aus dem 17. Jahrhundert.
Eigentlich hatten sie vorgehabt, eine Stadtvilla in Aix zu kaufen, um
Lillians umfangreiche Kostümsammlung unterbringen zu können.
Historische Kostüme, vor allem aus dem 18. Jahrhundert, sind Lillians
Leidenschaft, und Stücke aus ihrer Sammlung gingen schon als
Leihgabe an verschiedene Museen. Begeistert von den anmutigen
Proportionen, der hübschen Treppenanlage auf der Gartenseite und
der klassischen italienischen Gartenanlage mit Brunnen und Terrassen kauften sie den Besitz, und Lillian übernahm es, ihn wieder in
eine perfekte »folie« des 18. Jahrhunderts zu verwandeln. Ihr Sinn für
Dramatik findet hier Ausdruck in der barocken Innenausstattung und
den kostümierten Schaufensterpuppen, die das provenzalische Leben
vor zweihundert Jahren verkörpern. Gerade die Faszination, die von
den alltäglichen Dingen, den Kleinigkeiten des täglichen Lebens aus-
geht – sie schreibt an einem Buch über das Phänomen des »quotidien«, des Alltäglichen –, zeichnet Lillians Sammlung aus und ver-
leiht ihr eine besondere Vitalität.

Above: a view of the classically appointed ornamental pond with a lavender field in the background – a reference to the Provençal countryside that was planted before the Williams bought the house.
Facing page: a view of what was originally a private theatre in the garden with a "tromp l'œil" in "azulejos".
On the following pages: a view of the "Salon des Chinoiseries", dominated by 18th-century terracotta statuettes of nodding mandarins and a late 17th-century Venetian harpsichord. The acid-yellow curtain silk was picked up from a dress manufacturer in Paris, as the right shade was simply not avaliable in furnishing fabric.

Ci-dessus: l'alignement classique du bassin et, derrière, un champ de lavande typiquement provençal qui était déjà là quand les Williams ont acheté la maison.
Page de droite: l'ancien petit théâtre privé dans le jardin, avec un trompe l'œil en azulejos.
Double page suivante: le «salon des chinoiseries», dominé par des statuettes de mandarins articulées en terre cuite datant du XVIIIe siècle et une harpe vénitienne de la fin du XVIIe siècle. Les rideaux en soie jaune acidulé ont été choisis chez un fabricant parisien d'étoffes de confection, la teinte désirée étant introuvable parmi les tissus d'ameublement.

Oben: Blick auf den klassisch angelegten Teich, im Hintergrund ein Lavendelfeld, ein beim Kauf bereits vorhandener Anklang an die provenzalische Landschaft.
Rechte Seite: Blick auf das ehemalige private Theater im Garten, das mit »Azulejo«-Kacheln in Trompe-l'œil-Technik ausgestattet ist.
Folgende Doppelseite: Blick in den »Salon des chinoiseries«, der von nickenden Mandarinen (Terrakottastatuen aus dem 18. Jahrhundert) und einem venezianischen Cembalo (aus dem späten 17. Jahrhundert) beherrscht wird. Die giftgelbe Vorhangseide wurde bei einer Kleiderfabrik in Paris gekauft, da es den richtigen Farbton als Dekostoff einfach nicht gab.

Above: *in the vaulted former stables, an arrangement of Neapolitan 18th-century nativity figures, and an architectural piece of the same period, probably also used in nativities. In the background, lifesized secular figures, that originally belonged to the Dukes of Bologna in the 16th century.*

Facing page, clockwise from top left: *a Louis XVI bed "à la Polonaise" frames a Provençal portrait of a girl; neatly tied bundles of "Le Mercure de France", the daily newspaper from the reign of Louis XIV; a King Charles spaniel on its very grand doggy bed; a detail of one of the mandarins in the Chinese salon.*

On the following pages: *a tent-like room, in striped fabric, entirely "Directoire", with further pieces from the impressive collection of antique musical instruments.*

Ci-dessus: *dans les anciennes écuries voûtées, une collection de santons napolitains du XVIIIe siècle et une maquette de la même époque, sans doute utilisée elle aussi dans les crèches. En arrière-plan, des statues grandeur nature qui appartenaient aux ducs de Bologne au XVIe siècle.*

Page de droite, en haut à gauche: *un lit Louis XVI à la polonaise dont le baldaquin encadre un portrait provençal de jeune fille; puis dans le sens des aiguilles d'une montre: des piles joliment nouées du «Mercure de France», un quotidien datant de Louis XIV; un king-charles sur une couche royale digne de lui; un des mandarins du salon chinois.*

Double page suivante: *un salon façon tente en tissu rayé, entièrement Directoire, et d'autres pièces de l'impressionnante collection d'instruments de musique anciens.*

Oben: *In den mit Gewölben versehenen ehemaligen Ställen sieht man ein Stilleben mit neapolitanischen Krippenfiguren aus dem 18. Jahrhundert und ein Architekturmodell aus der gleichen Epoche, das wahrscheinlich ebenfalls im Rahmen einer Krippe verwendet wurde. Im Hintergrund lebensgroße profane Figuren aus dem 16. Jahrhundert, die ursprünglich den Herzögen von Bologna gehörten.*

Rechte Seite, im Uhrzeigersinn von links oben: *Ein Louis-Seize-Baldachinbett umrahmt das Porträt eines provenzalischen Mädchens; sauber gebündelte Ausgaben des »Mercure de France«, einer Tageszeitung aus der Zeit Ludwigs XIV.; einer von mehreren King-Charles-Spaniels in seinem überaus prunkvollen Himmelbett; einer der Mandarine aus dem chinesischen Salon.*

Folgende Doppelseite: *ein zeltartiger, mit gestreiftem Stoff vollständig im Directoire-Stil eingerichteter Salon mit weiteren Stücken der eindrucksvollen Sammlung alter Musikinstrumente.*

Facing page: A Baroque marble sink dominates a luxuriously appointed "cabinet de toilette" in pistachio and pale rose that features a gold vermeil bath, made for the famous Parisian courtesan who was mistress of the Prince of Wales in the late 19th century.
Above: Lillian William's pink bedroom. The fabric was specially commissioned from Manuel Canovas and based on an 18th-century design from her extensive collection.

Page de gauche: Un lavabo baroque en marbre domine le luxueux cabinet de toilette pistache et rose pâle. La baignoire en vermeil fut fabriquée pour une célèbre courtisane parisienne, maîtresse du Prince de Galles à la fin du XIXe siècle.
Ci-dessus: la chambre rose de Lillian Williams. Le tissu, commandé spécialement chez Manuel Canovas, reproduit un motif dix-huitième de la collection de costumes de la maîtresse de maison.

Linke Seite: Ein barockes Marmorwaschbecken beherrscht das luxuriös, pistaziengrün und blaßrosa ausgestattete »Cabinet de toilette«, zu dem auch eine vergoldete Email-Badewanne gehört. Sie wurde für die berühmte Pariser Kurtisane angefertigt, die im späten 19. Jahrhundert Mätresse des Prinzen von Wales war.
Oben: Lillians rosa Schlafzimmer. Der Stoff wurde eigens bei Manuel Canovas gefertigt und greift ein Muster des 18. Jahrhunderts aus ihrer umfangreichen Sammlung auf.

The gracious property Domaine de Souviou is situated at the foot of the mountainous Sainte-Baume, between Aix-en-Provence and Toulon. When the Cagnolaris first visited, it was a pile of ruins. Despite their busy Parisian life, and with the help of the architect Xavier Tronel and the decorator Patrice Nourissat, the house has now been restored to its former glory. The walls and ceilings were given rounded contours, the inside was painted olive, ochre and cream, wooden floors and floor-tiles were laid and a large dining-room-cum-kitchen installed, along with several bathrooms. The grounds have become fruitful once again and produce not only three different fine olive oils but also red, white and rosé Bandol wine under the label of the property. After almost ten years of work on the estate, the Cagnolaris have even fulfilled their pet ambition: to produce a "grand cru", a noble wine aged in their own cellars.

Christiane et Serge Cagnolari

La première fois que les Cagnolari ont visité l'élégant Domaine de Souviou, situé au pied du massif de la Sainte-Baume, entre Aix-en-Provence et Toulon, il n'était plus qu'un tas de ruines. En dépit de leur vie parisienne fort chargée, et avec l'aide de l'architecte Xavier Tronel et du décorateur Patrice Nourissat, ils lui ont redonné sa splendeur d'autrefois. Les contours des murs et des plafonds ont été arrondis, l'intérieur a été peint en vert olive, ocre et blanc cassé, les sols ont été recouverts de parquets ou de tomettes, une grande cuisine-salle à manger a été créée, ainsi que plusieurs salles de bains. La terre a retrouvé sa fertilité d'antan et produit, outre trois sortes d'excellentes huiles d'olive, du Bandol rosé, blanc et rouge qui porte le nom du domaine. Après dix années de travail sur la propriété, les Cagnolari ont enfin réalisé un de leurs rêves: produire un grand cru qui vieillisse dans leur propres caves.

Das schöne Anwesen Domaine de Souviou liegt am Fuß des Sainte-Baume-Massivs zwischen Aix-en-Provence und Toulon. Als die Cagnolaris das Haus zum erstenmal besichtigten, war es eine einzige Ruine, doch ihrem anstrengendem Pariser Leben zum Trotz sorgten sie mit Hilfe des Architekten Xavier Tronel und des Innenausstatters Patrice Nourissat dafür, daß es in seiner früheren Pracht wieder auferstehen durfte. Wände und Decken wurden abgerundet, das Innere olivgrün, ocker und cremefarben gestrichen, Holzdielen und »tommette«-Fliesen gelegt und eine große Wohnküche sowie mehrere Badezimmer geschaffen. Auch der Erdboden ringsherum wurde wieder fruchtbar gemacht und liefert nicht nur drei verschiedene edle Olivenöle, sondern darüber hinaus Bandol-Wein in Rot, Weiß und Rosé, der unter dem Namen des Gutes verkauft wird. Nach fast zehnjähriger Arbeit auf dem Anwesen ist es den Cagnolaris sogar gelungen, ihr ehrgeizigstes Vorhaben zu verwirklichen: einen Grand Cru zu produzieren, einen wahrhaft noblen, in ihrem eigenen Keller gereiften Wein.

Previous pages and above: *views of the garden, which is delicately pretty and generously planted with a wealth of Mediterranean flowering plants and trees.*
Facing page: *the table set for lunch under the "tonelle".*
Right: *a detail of the "Domaine de Souviou" wines and the oils produced by the century-old olive trees in the grounds.*

Pages précédentes et ci-dessus: *différentes vues du jardin, d'une beauté délicate et accueillant une abondance de plantes à fleurs et d'arbres méditerranéens.*
Page de gauche: *le déjeuner servi sous la tonnelle.*
A droite: *les vins du «Domaine de Souviou» et les huiles produites par les oliviers centenaires.*

Vorhergehende Seiten und oben: *Ansichten des Gartens, der ausnehmend hübsch hergerichtet und üppig mit mediterranen Gewächsen und Bäumen bepflanzt ist.*
Linke Seite: *Unter der Laube ist der Tisch für das Mittagessen gedeckt.*
Rechts: *Einige der Weine der »Domaine de Souviou« und ihrer Öle, die aus den Früchten der eigenen jahrhundertealten Olivenbäume gepreßt werden.*

Above and facing page: *two views of the ochre and olive master bedroom. The frieze on the wall evokes Piero della Francesca, and indeed the atmosphere recalls that of an Italian "palazzo".*
Detail bottom right: *the bathroom designed by Xavier Tronel, with its tiled terracotta floor. The stone in which the sinks and the bath have been fitted has been treated with linseed oil. The three pine-framed mirrors add to the graphic impact of the room.*
On the following pages: *the welcoming kitchen, one of the key rooms in the house. Designed by Patrice Nourissat and built in tinted pine by a local craftsman, the main piece of furniture is a large farmhouse table around which family and friends congregate for informal meals.*

Ci-dessus et page de droite: *la chambre de maître vert olive et ocre. La frise à la Piero della Francesca et l'atmosphère générale évoquent un «palazzo» italien.*
Détail ci-dessous à droite: *la salle de bains dessinée par Xavier Tronel, avec son sol carrelé en terre cuite. Le lavabo et la baignoire ont été insérés dans une pierre traitée à l'huile de lin. Les trois miroirs avec un cadre en bois de pin ajoutent encore à l'effet géométrique du décor.*
Double page suivante: *la chaleureuse cuisine, l'une des pièces maîtresses de la maison. Au centre, une grande table de ferme, dessinée par Patrice Nourissat et réalisée en pin teinté par un artisan de la région. C'est autour d'elle que s'assoient la famille et les amis pour des repas à la bonne franquette.*

Oben und rechte Seite: *zwei Ansichten des ocker und olivgrün gestrichenen Schlafzimmers. Der Wandfries erinnert an Piero della Francesca, die ganze Atmosphäre läßt an einen italienischen Palazzo denken.*
Detail unten rechts: *das von Xavier Tronel gestaltete Badezimmer mit Terrakotta-Bodenfliesen. Der Stein, aus dem die Waschbecken*

und die Wanne geschnitten sind, wurde mit Leinöl behandelt. Die drei in Kiefer gerahmten Spiegel unterstreichen die graphische Ausdruckskraft des Raumes.
Folgende Doppelseite: *die einladende Küche, einer der wichtigsten Räume des Hauses. Sie wurde von Patrice Nourissat entworfen und von einem hiesigen Handwerker in lasierter Kiefer gearbeitet. Beherrschendes Möbelstück ist der große Bauerntisch, an dem sich Familie und Freunde zu zwanglosen Mahlzeiten einfinden.*

Above: the garden façade showing the turrets which were added in the 19th century.
Left: the pool and the poolhouse, both designed by Louis-Charles de Rémusat.

Ci-dessus: la façade côté jardin, avec ses tourelles rajoutées au XIXe siècle.
A gauche: la piscine et la cabine de bain, toutes deux dessinées par Louis-Charles de Rémusat.

Oben: die Gartenfassade mit den im 19. Jahrhundert hinzugefügten Ecktürmchen.
Links: der Swimmingpool mit dem Umkleidehäuschen, beides nach Entwürfen von Louis-Charles de Rémusat gebaut.

"My Father's Castle": Louis-Charles de Rémusat refers to the family property with an appropiate veiled reference to the title of one of Pagnol's best-loved books about Provence. The chateau is a splendid 18th-century construction that was acquired by the late father Rémusat just after the last war. With a rare sensibility he decided not to tear out the interiors but to leave all the 19th-century decoration, including wall hangings, upholstery and curtains, in place. Such a gesture of deference towards the building's gracious and aristocratic past has allowed the chateau, thus preserved, to age gracefully, as if lost in time. Louis-Charles, who trained as an architect, has restored and modernized the extensive outbuildings, making the property a real family home where the Rémusats all gather for Christmas and the long summer holidays.

«Le château de mon père»

Cette allusion au titre de l'un des plus beaux romans de Pagnol sur la Provence prend tout son sens dans la bouche de Louis-Charles de Rémusat lorsqu'il parle de sa propriété de famille. Le château en question est une splendide demeure du XVIIIe siècle achetée par feu monsieur de Rémusat père juste après la dernière guerre. Avec une sensibilité rare, celui-ci a décidé de conserver la décoration du XIXe siècle, y compris tentures murales, tissus d'ameublement et rideaux. Grâce à ce respect pour son passé élégant et aristocratique, le château a gardé intact toute sa grâce d'autrefois. Louis-Charles, qui a une formation d'architecte, a restauré et modernisé les nombreuses dépendances, transformant la propriété en une véritable maison de famille où les Rémusat se retrouvent à chaque Noël et pour les grandes vacances.

»Das Schloß meines Vaters«: Louis-Charles de Rémusat bezeichnet seinen Familiensitz in Anlehnung an den Titel eines der beliebtesten Provence-Bände Marcel Pagnols augenzwinkernd als »Schloß meines Vaters«. Der Herrensitz ist ein prachtvolles Gebäude aus dem 18. Jahrhundert, das der verstorbene Monsieur Rémusat senior kurz nach dem zweiten Weltkrieg kaufte. Mit seltenem Feingefühl beschloß er, die Innenausstattung nicht herauszureißen, sondern die gesamte Dekoration aus dem 19. Jahrhundert einschließlich der Wandbehänge, Polster und Vorhänge beizubehalten. Dank solcher Ehrfurcht vor einer anmutigen, aristokratischen Vergangenheit war es dem Gebäude vergönnt, in Frieden zu altern, als sei es der Zeit entflohen. Louis-Charles, von Beruf Architekt, erneuerte und modernisierte die weitläufigen Nebengebäude und machte den Besitz zu einem echten Heim der Rémusats, in dem sich alle Familienmitglieder jedes Jahr zu Weihnachten und in den langen Sommerferien einfinden.

Page 271: The giant red plantpot, a sculpted piece by Jean-Pierre Raynaud, dominates the grounds, a sculpture park showcasing some of Navarra's most important pieces.
Above: the salon in the guest-house. The piece on the left is by Le Gac. The round painting on the far wall is by Tom Wesselmann.
Facing page: the pool room. In the foreground a Le Corbusier "chaise-longue", in the background a piece of Oceanic primitive art, and a smaller sculpture by Raynaud.

Page 271: Un gigantesque pot de fleur, sculpture de Jean-Pierre Raynaud, domine la propriété, un parc de sculptures où sont exposées quelques-unes des plus belles pièces de Navarra.
Ci-dessus: le salon de la maison d'amis. Le tableau à gauche est de Le Gac. La toile ronde sur le mur du fond est signée Tom Wesselmann.
Page de droite: le coin «salon» de la piscine intérieure. Au premier plan, une chaise longue de Le Corbusier et au fond, une sculpture primitive océanienne et une autre, plus petite, de Raynaud.

Page 271: Der riesige rote Blumentopf ist eine Plastik Jean-Pierre Raynauds. Er beherrscht das Grundstück, das eigentlich ein Skulpturenpark mit einigen von Navarras bedeutendsten Stücken ist.
Oben: der Salon im Gästehaus. Das Werk links stammt von Le Gac. Das runde Gemälde an der rückwärtigen Wand ist ein Tom Wesselmann.
Rechte Seite: der Vorraum des Swimmingpools. Im Vordergrund eine Liege von Le Corbusier, im Hintergrund eine primitive Plastik aus Ozeanien und eine kleinere Arbeit von Raynaud.

Detail right: *the bed designed by Mario Botta with a monumental painting by Jean-Michel Basquiat as a headboard.*
Below: *a view of the "wall of images" in front of the bed in the master bedroom. The painting in the background is a Christo avant-project for the wrapping of the Reichstag.*

Détail de droite: *le lit dessiné par Mario Botta avec une peinture monumentale de Jean-Michel Basquiat en guise de tête de lit.*
Ci-dessous: *le «mur d'images» devant le lit de la chambre de maître. La peinture en arrière-plan est un avant-projet de Christo pour l'emballage du Reichstag.*

Detail rechts: *das von Mario Botta entworfene Bett, dem ein monumentales Gemälde von Jean-Michel Basquiat als Kopfteil dient.*
Unten: *ein Blick auf die »Bilderwand« vor dem Bett im Schlafzimmer. Das Gemälde im Hintergrund ist ein Vorentwurf von Christo für die Verhüllung des Berliner Reichstages.*

Above: *a view of the corridor, with the three-dimensional sculptures by Charles Simmonds niched in the wall itself. These are detailed miniature landscapes in mud, earth and tiny bricks, assembled by the artist on site with tweezers and other tools of the miniature trade.*
Following pages: *the indoor swimming pool, in "pietra serena", an Italian volcanic rock. The furniture is by Le Corbusier, and the room contains pieces by James Brown, Jenny Holzer and Raynaud. The statuettes are examples of primitive art.*

Ci-dessus: *le couloir, avec des sculptures tridimensionnelles de Charles Simmonds nichées directement dans le mur. Ces petits paysages faits avec de la boue, de la terre et de minuscules briques ont été assemblés sur place par l'artiste, avec des pinces à épiler et autres instruments de miniaturiste.*
Double page suivante: *la piscine intérieure en «pietra serena», une roche volcanique italienne. Les sièges sont de Le Corbusier. La salle abrite des œuvres de James Brown, Jenny Holzer et Raynaud, et des statuettes d'art primitif.*

Oben: *Blick in den Flur, wo Charles Simmonds dreidimensionale Plastiken direkt in die Wand eingearbeitet sind. Es handelt sich um detaillierte Miniaturlandschaften aus Schlamm, Erde und winzigen Ziegeln, die der Künstler an Ort und Stelle mit Hilfe einer Pinzette und anderer winziger Werkzeuge zusammengesetzt hat.*
Folgende Doppelseite: *Der Swimmingpool aus »pietra serena«, einem italienischen Vulkangestein. Die Sitzmöbel sind von Le Corbusier, darüber hinaus enthält der Raum Werke von James Brown, Jenny Holzer und Raynaud. Die Statuetten sind Beispiele primitiver Volkskunst.*

Not far from Saint-Paul-de-Vence, the picturesque hill village that has been Provence's leading artists' colony since the 1920s, lies a strictly contemporary "folie": the house of the painter and sculptor Arman. In his work, Arman has always exalted the object, transposing it from its proper place in our lives and thus transforming it into an object of art. When designing his house, he applied the same principle. Thus, strange and apparently unclassifiable items that on closer inspection turn out to be old and familiar friends such as springs, drums, telephones or sewing machines, have been used as building materials to produce a home which is a baffling challenge to conventional decorative principles. It might shock, it might charm or amuse, but this is one Provençal house that is light-years from the traditional country "mas".

Arman

Non loin de Saint-Paul-de-Vence, pittoresque village à flanc de colline devenu la plus importante colonie d'artistes de Provence dans les années vingt, se trouve une «folie» d'une modernité absolue: la maison du peintre et sculpteur Arman. Arman a toujours sublimé l'objet dans son œuvre, le sortant de son contexte pour en faire un «objet d'art». Pour concevoir sa maison, il a appliqué le même principe. Des objets étranges et apparemment inclassables, mais qui, vus de plus près, s'avèrent être de vieux compagnons familiers tels que ressorts, tambours, téléphones ou machines à coudre, ont servi de matériaux de construction, produisant un effet aux antipodes des principes conventionnels de la décoration. La maison peut choquer, charmer ou amuser, mais une chose est sûre: elle se situe à des années-lumière du «mas» provençal traditionnel.

Nicht weit entfernt von dem malerischen Bergdorf Saint-Paul-de-Vence, das seit den zwanziger Jahren als führende Künstlerkolonie der Provence gilt, steht das moderne, extravagante Haus des Malers und Bildhauers Arman. Bei seiner Arbeit geht es Arman stets um Objekte, die er ihrem alltäglichen Platz in unserem Leben entreißt und sie in Kunstwerke verwandelt. Bei der Planung seines Hauses wandte er dasselbe Verfahren an: Es wimmelt von eigenartigen, scheinbar undefinierbaren Dingen, die sich auf den zweiten Blick als gute alte Bekannte zu erkennen geben, seien es Sprungfedern, Waschmaschinentrommeln, Telefone oder Nähmaschinen. Sie sind Baumaterialien für ein Gebäude von verblüffender Eigenart, das konventionelle Dekorationsprinzipien auf den Kopf stellt. Mag man das Haus schockierend, ansprechend oder witzig finden, es ist jedenfalls meilenweit entfernt vom traditionellen provenzalischen Landhaus, dem »mas«.

Above and facing page: *two views of Lartigue's painting studio. The folding campbed and gay patchwork quilt, and indeed the simplicity with which the whole house is furnished, do not betray Lartigue's wealthy origins. The walls were painted at random in a swirling, colourful pattern. In fact, Lartigue used the wall to clean his paintbrush everytime he took a break. Florette vowed to keep the studio intact and indeed no changes have been made since Lartigue's death.*

Ci-dessus et page de droite: *l'atelier de Lartigue. Comme le décor humble de la maison attenante, le lit de camp et l'édredon en patchwork aux couleurs gaies ne témoignent pas des origines aisées de Lartigue. Les murs ont été peints à grands coups de pinceaux dans un tourbillon de couleurs. Pendant ses pauses, Lartigue y essuyait même ses pinceaux. Florette s'est promis de conserver cet atelier tel quel et, de fait, rien n'a changé depuis la mort de l'artiste.*

Oben und rechte Seite: *zwei Ansichten von Lartigues Atelier. Das Feldbett mit der fröhlichen Patchworkdecke und vor allem die Schlichtheit, mit der das ganze Haus eingerichtet ist, täuschen über Lartigues wohlhabende Herkunft hinweg. Die Wände sind nach dem Zufallsprinzip mit wirbelnden bunten Mustern bemalt. Lartigue strich nämlich an der Wand seine Pinsel ab, bevor er Pause machte. Florette versprach, das Atelier unangetastet zu lassen, und so ist seit Lartigues Tod nicht das geringste daran verändert worden.*

Adresses et sélection de brocantes
Addresses and selected "brocantes"
Adressen und ausgewählte »Brocantes«

Château d'Ansouis
Museum
Résidence des Ducs de
Sabran-Pontevès
84240 Ansouis

Henri Aubanel-Baroncelli
Horse Riding
Lou Simbèu
Route d'Aigues-Mortes,
Clos du Rhône
13460 Les Saintes-Maries-
de-la-Mer

Anna Bonde &
Arne Tengblad
Decoration
Quartier Bel Air
84220 Goult

Marie-Christine Cagnolari
Vineyard
Domaine de Souviou
RN 8
83330 Le Beausset

Bruno Carles
Shop
209–235 avenue de Lattre
de Tassigny
34400 Lunel

Denis Colomb
Architecture & Design
8 place Adolphe Max
75008 Paris

Denys Colomb de Daunant
Hotel
Le Mas de Cacharel
13460 Les Saintes-Maries-
de-la-Mer

Nasrine Faghih
Architecture
3 rue Chapon
75003 Paris

Emile Garcin
Estate Agency
8 boulevard Mirabeau
13210 Saint-Rémy-de-
Provence

Jacques Grange
Interior Decoration
118 rue du Faubourg-St.-
Honoré
75008 Paris

Michel Klein
Fashion
6 rue du Prè-aux-Clercs
75007 Paris

Enrico Navarra
Modern Art Gallery
16 avenue Matignon
75008 Paris

Xavier Nicod
Antiques
9 avenue des Quatre
Otages
84800 L'Isle-sur-la-Sorgue

Gerald Pellen
Horse Breeding
Mas les grandes Bouisses
13150 Boulbon

Jennifer &
Jean-Marie Rocchia
Provençal Honey and
Truffels
Campagne le Prince
13100 Beaurecueil

Château Unang
Hotel
Marie-Hélène &
Jean-Albert Lefer
Route de Méthanis
84570 Malemort-du-
Comtat

"Brocante" shops:

Fan'Broc
22 boulevard Mirabeau
Saint-Rémy-de-Provence

Philippe Eckert
Ebène
38 boulevard Victor Hugo
Saint-Rémy-de-Provence

Sous L'Olivier
7 boulevard Mirabeau
Saint-Rémy-de-Provence

Catherine & Michel Biehn
Espace Béchard
1 avenue Jean Charmasson
L'Isle-sur-la-Sorgue

Christine &
Denis Nossereau
7 avenue des Quatre
Otages
L'Isle-sur-la-Sorgue

Hervé Baume
19 rue de la Petite-Fusterie
Avignon

Hôtel Nord-Pinus
6 rue du Palais
Arles

"Brocante" markets:

Arles: Boulevard des Lices
on the first Wednesday of
the month

Avignon: Place Crillon on
Saturday mornings
Place des Carmes on
Sunday mornings

L'Isle-sur-la-Sorgue:
Avenue des Quatre Otages
on Saturday and Sunday

Marseille: Cours Julien on
the second Sunday of the
month

Bibliographie / Bibliography

Agulhon, Maurice: *The Republic in the Village. The People of the Var from the French Revolution to the Second Republic*, Cambridge, 1982

Aubanel, Henri: *Je suis Manadier*, Editions du Conquistador, 1957

Bicknell, C.: *The Prehistoric Rock Engravings in the Italian Maritime Alps*, Bordighera, 1902

Borgé, Jacques, and Nicolas Viasnoff: *Archives de Provence*, Editions Michèle Trinkville, 1994

Chabot, Jacques: *La Provence de Giono*, Aix-en-Provence, 1982

Curnier, Pierre: *La Haute-Provence dans les lettres françaises*, Chantemerle Editeur, 1973

D'Agay, Frédéric: *La Provence des châteaux et des bastides*, Editions du Chêne, 1991

David, Elizabeth: *French Provincial Cooking*, London, 1960

Desaule, Pierre: *Les Bories de Vaucluse*, Paris, 1976

Deux, Pierre, Pierre Moulin, Pierre Le Vec and Linda Dannenberg: *L'Art de vivre en Provence*, Flammarion, 1987

Durrell, Lawrence: *Caesar's Vast Ghost*, faber and faber, 1990

Eydoux, Henri-Paul: *Promenades en Provence*, Editions André Balland, 1969

Lady Fortescue: *Perfume from Provence*, London, 1935

Ford, Ford Madox: *Provence. From Minstrels to the Machine*, London, 1935

Giono, Jean: *Provence*, Paris, 1957

– *Provence perdue*, Paris, 1967

Hare, Augustus: *The Rivieras*, London, 1897

Hennessy, James Pope: *Aspects of Provence*, London, 1952

Hughes, John: *An Itinerary in Provence and the Rhône*, London, 1822

Jacobs, Michael: *A Guide to Provence*, Penguin, 1988

James, Henry: *A Little Tour in France*, Penguin Travel Library, 1985

Jouveau, R.: *Histoire du Félibrige*, 1976

Legré, L.: *Le Poète Théodore Aubanel, Récit d'un témoin de sa vie*, Paris, 1984

Magnan, Pierre, and Daniel Faure: *Les Promenades de Jean Giono*, Editions du Chêne, 1994

Massot, J.-L.: *Maisons rurales et vie paysanne en Provence*, Ivry, 1975

Mauron, Marie: *Quand la Provence nous est contée*, Presses Pocket, 1975

Merimée, Prosper: *Notes d'un voyage dans le Midi de France*, Paris, 1835

Mermod, Françoise: *La Provence. Peintres et écrivains de Théophile Gautier à Paul Valéry, de Corot à Dufy*, Edition Mermod, 1956

Mistral, Frédéric: *Memoirs of Mistral*, London, 1907

Mouriès, Nathalie: *Guide Provence de charme*, Editions Rivage, 1994

Pagnol, Marcel: *La Gloire de mon père*, Paris, 1957

– *Le Château de ma mère*, Paris, 1958

– *Le Temps des secrets*, Paris, 1960

Pickvance, R.: *Van Gogh in Arles*, New York, 1984

Olivier-Elliot, Patrick: *Lubéron, carnets d'un voyageur attentif*, Editions Edisud, 1991

Petrarch: *L'Ascension du Mont Ventoux*, Editions Séquences, 1990

Reboul, J.-B.: *La Cuisinière provençale*, Marseille, 1895

Silvester, Hans, and Jean-Paul Clébert: *Tsiganes et gitanes*, Editions du Chêne, 1974

Stendhal: *Journal d'un voyage dans le midi de France*, Paris, 1858

Sussex, R.T.: *Henri Bosco: A Study of the Novels*, London, 1966

Vergé, Roger: *Cuisine of the Sun*, London, 1979

Remerciements / Acknowledgements / Danksagungen

This book would not have been possible without the help of my friends and advisors Anna Davenport, Elisabeth Kime and Kathy Korvin who all contributed greatly to the project.
Erica Lennard, Denis Colomb, Phillipe Seuillet, Jacques Grange, Marianne Haas, Nicholas Barrera, Nicole de Vesian, Marie-Colette and Jean Michel Borgeaud, Marie-Madeleine Nelson, Marilse de Font-Reaulx and especially Guilleaume de Laubier made the production of this book a reality with their help and advice.
The following stylists and magazines deserve credit for their productions which they kindly allowed us to reproduce: Bruno Carles was styled by Christine Grange-Bary for "Maison et Jardin"; Guillemette Goëlff was styled by Florence Beaufre; Michel Klein was styled by Marie Dahadie for "Maison et Jardin"; Xavier Nicod was styled by Anne-Marie Comte for "Marie Claire Maison"; Jacques Henri Lartigue was styled by Bibi Gex for "Elle Deco"; Arne Tengblad, Daniel Vial, Lillian Williams, Enrico Navarra, Arman and Le facteur à cheval were styled by Philippe Seuillet. The text background for La maison d'un marchand d'art came from Christine Lippens. Nicole de Vesian was styled by Sonia Dieudonné for "Maison et Jardin"; Le château de mon père was styled by Chris O'Byrne; Christiane et Serge Cagnolari was styled by Christine Grange-Bary for "Maison et Jardin", Nasrine Faghih was styled byGilles Dalliers for "Maison Française"; Franck Pascal et Marc Heracle was styled by Joëlle Balaresque for "Maison et Jardin".
Special thanks to Charles-Henri de L. for helping me with the manuscript in its final stages and for creating the conditions in which I could write.
This book is for my mother who first awoke my love of Provence.

Lisa Lovatt-Smith

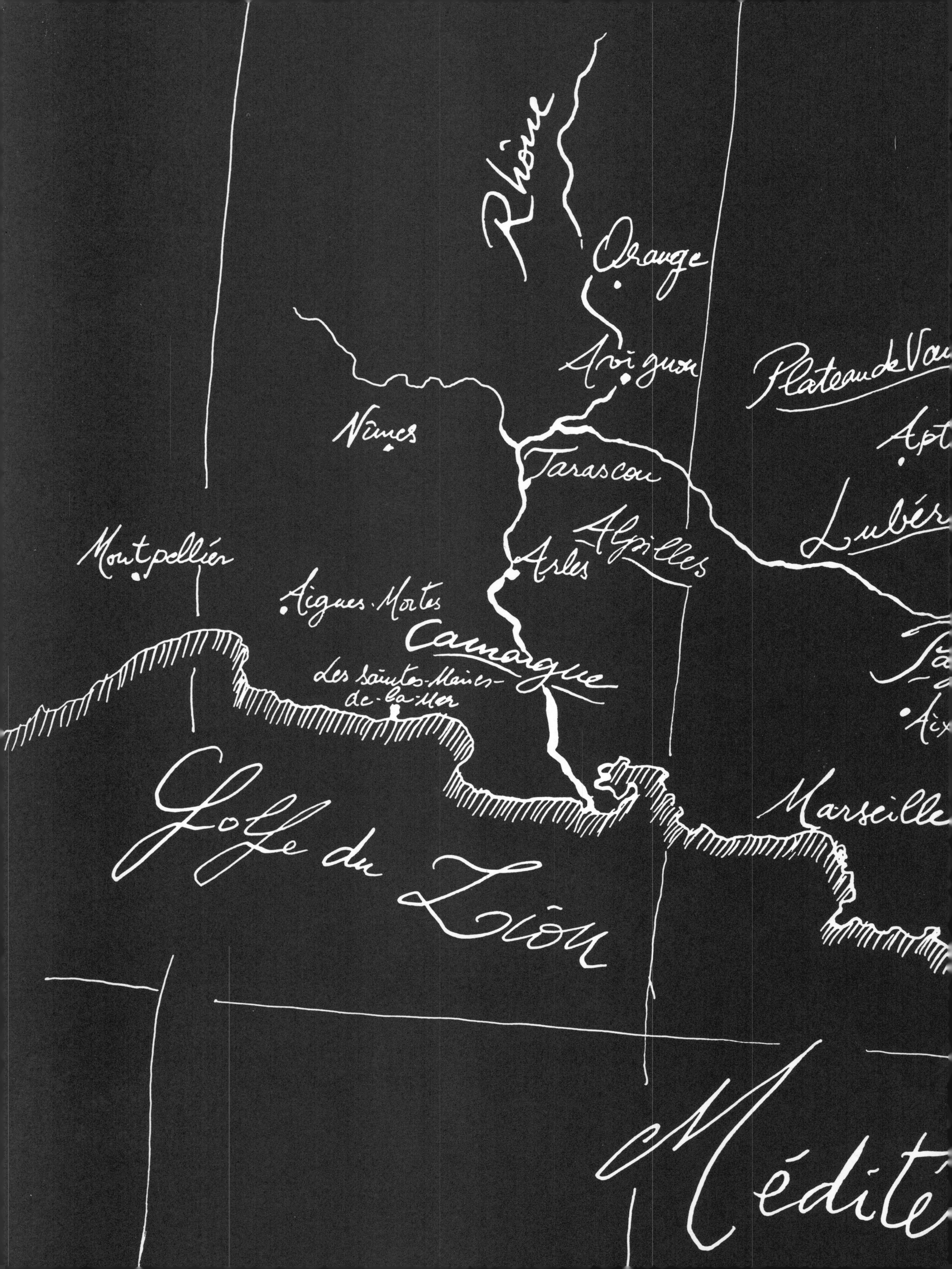

Rhône
Orange
Avignon
Plateau de Vau
Nîmes
Apt
Tarascon
Lubér
Alpilles
Montpellier
Arles
Aigues-Mortes
Camargue
Les Saintes-Maries-de-la-Mer
Aix
Marseille
Golfe du Lion
Médite